T0303346

A Preliminary Assessment of the Regionally Aligned Forces (RAF) Concept's Implications for Army Personnel Management

M. Wade Markel, Bryan W. Hallmark, Peter Schirmer,
Louay Constant, Jaime L. Hastings, Henry A. Leonard,
Kristin J. Leuschner, Lauren A. Mayer, Caolionn O'Connell,
Christina Panis, Jose R. Rodriguez, Lisa Saum-Manning,
Jonathan Welch

Prepared for the United States Army

Approved for public release; distribution unlimited

For more information on this publication, visit www.rand.org/t/rr1065

Library of Congress Control Number: 2015955340

ISBN 978-0-8330-9064-5

Published by the RAND Corporation, Santa Monica, Calif.

© Copyright 2015 RAND Corporation

RAND® is a registered trademark.

Support RAND
Make a tax-deductible charitable contribution at
www.rand.org/giving/contribute

www.rand.org

Preface

This report documents research conducted as part of the project "Manpower and Professional Development Implications of the Regionally Aligned Forces (RAF) Concept." This project's purpose was to help the U.S. Army adapt its personnel and manpower management systems to support the RAF concept while continuing to develop leaders' capabilities to conduct unified land operations worldwide.

The report reviews the RAF concept and the limited state of the Army's experience implementing it. It estimates the potential scope and scale of the requirement for regional expertise; assesses the Army's ability to develop the required number of soldiers; and recommends changes to the goals, objectives, and criteria that the Army's personnel management system uses to match soldiers who have expertise to the positions requiring it and to develop soldiers with that expertise. Because the Army has acquired relatively little experience implementing RAF, significant changes to the personnel system would be premature. Rather, we recommend that the Army leverage its adoption of talent management to meet RAF demands as they emerge and are clarified through operational experience so they can be translated into objectives and criteria for personnel managers. This report should be of interest to Army officials in the personnel and force management communities.

This research was sponsored by Anthony J. Stamilio, Deputy Assistant Secretary of the Army for Civilian Personnel and Quality of Life, and MG Thomas C. Seamands, director of Military Personnel Management, U.S. Army Deputy Chief of Staff for Personnel (G-1), and conducted within the RAND Arroyo Center's Personnel, Training, and Health Program. RAND Arroyo Center, part of the RAND Corporation, is a federally funded research and development center sponsored by the United States Army.

The Project Unique Identification Code (PUIC) for the project that produced this document is HQD146655.

Contents

Figures

Tables

Summary

To enhance relationships among Army, joint, and other relevant planning staffs at the regional level and to improve Army units' familiarity with and expertise regarding areas in which they are likely to be employed, the Army is implementing the Regionally Aligned Forces (RAF) concept. Beyond competence in region-specific languages and culture, additional knowledge, skills, abilities, and other characteristics (KSAOs) might be needed in particular regional contexts. The assumption underlying the RAF concept is that different regions' characteristics constrain military operations in different ways. For example, the state of regional economic development affects the degree of contract support available and, thus, operational sustainment concepts of operation. Different national rules governing use of the electronic spectrum limit Army forces' use of certain capabilities. Desert or littoral geography affects operational maneuver. These are just a few examples. These competencies and their development mean that the successful execution of military operations under RAF will affect and be affected by the balance of breadth and depth of Army leaders' operational experience. However, the Army's ability to identify and track such KSAOs throughout soldiers' careers is limited and constrained. Thus, although regional alignment appears to have potential implications for leader development and personnel management, the magnitude and direction of these implications have yet to be identified.

Moreover, the Army must contemplate these trade-offs under conditions of considerable uncertainty about the nature and extent of operational demand in each region, the KSAOs that soldiers might need to help Army forces respond to those demands, and the positions for which such KSAOs will be needed. Army forces' experience in conducting the range of military operations in the array of countries envisioned under RAF has been limited. Stakeholders have a range of opinions on the nature of regional expertise required and its value in achieving mission objectives. To date, there has been little systematic, empirical analysis of those issues.

Accordingly, the Assistant Secretary of the Army for Manpower and Reserve Affairs and the U.S. Army Deputy Chief of Staff for Personnel (G-1) asked the RAND Arroyo Center to help the Army adapt its personnel and manpower management systems to support the RAF concept while continuing to develop leaders' capabilities to conduct unified land operations worldwide.

Research Approach

The concept of expertise underpinned our investigation. We use the term *regional expertise* to connote the combination of education and experience required for effective performance in a particular regional context. Although language and cultural proficiency are usually elements of regional expertise, the concept focuses on those KSAOs that improve Army forces' effectiveness in different regional contexts. Practitioners must understand how the regional context constrains, limits, and sometimes enables military operations. For example, national rules on the use of the electromagnetic spectrum might limit the use or effectiveness of certain communication and electronic devices. The state of economic development in a given region should shape the logistic support plan. Given the link between regional and functional expertise, it seems clear that the nature and degree of regional expertise required will vary with the region and position in question.

Regional expertise differs from functional expertise. For the purpose of this report, we define functional expertise as the ability to perform the specific tasks required by a soldier's military occupational specialty (MOS) or area of concentration in any environment. Fire support planning is an example of a domain of functional expertise. Regional expertise consists of knowing how, for example, operating in Africa affects fire support planning.

For purposes of this analysis, we equate regions with combatant command areas of responsibility (AORs). The Unified Command Plan establishes combatant command AORs based on common operational characteristics, the most important of which is contiguous geography. Although combatant command AORs contain several distinct subregions, we assume for this analysis that they share enough in common to make regional expertise a meaningful domain.

This expertise can result from any number of different combinations of education and experience. Education can be formal, provided through military or civilian institutions, or the result of self-study, writing, and reflection. Useful experience could include military deployments, study abroad, or training in an environment that effectively simulates the region in question. In fact, soldiers who are immigrants or the children of immigrants might well enter the Army with the relevant linguistic and cultural expertise. Use of the term *expertise* does not indicate that soldiers need to become "experts." Instead, we use the term *expertise* to connote significantly increased understanding of a region's dynamics—and how those dynamics should shape military operations—that are operationally useful. The nature and degree of expertise required will differ by the position.

Our analysis focuses on experience—specifically, assignments—for several reasons. First, there is an internal Army effort already looking at changes to Army education and training whose work we did not wish to duplicate. Second, experience is a reasonable, measurable proxy for expertise. The number of soldiers with repeated assignments aligned with a particular region approximates the number of experts in the operationally relevant dynamics of that region. The major question that RAF's instantiation poses for personnel management is whether providing the required number of such soldiers with the right level of such expertise requires habitually aligning most career soldiers with particular regions. Third, the academic literature indicates that experience plays the dominant role in the development of expertise. There are, of course, multiple paths to obtaining the relevant experience.

A research approach focused on experience will not be perfect. On the one hand, assignment to a regionally aligned unit might not actually produce relevant experience or expertise. On the other hand, many soldiers might have developed relevant expertise outside of the military. However imperfect, experience or potential experience is the best proxy for expertise available to us *for the purposes of our analysis*, especially for simulating the development of expertise over the length of a soldier's career. Ergo, we focused our efforts on assessing both potential requirements for soldiers with regional *expertise* and the Army's ability to provide soldiers with an appropriate level of *experience* to meet those requirements. That does not mean that we think that military assignments are the only way to obtain relevant expertise in the real world.

Our research method included three components, as described in the rest of this section.

Estimating the Potential Scope and Scale of Personnel Requirements

In order to support RAF, the Army's personnel management system must provide enough soldiers with the right combination of education and experience to meet operational requirements. Consequently, we began by assessing the potential scope (the kinds of positions for which some degree of regional expertise is required) and scale (the number of such positions) of these requirements. Providing those soldiers might involve trade-offs and, consequently, risk. Increasing soldiers' regional expertise might require accepting risk with regard to their functional expertise. Managing soldiers' careers to increase their exposure to particular regions might incur risk with regard to other personnel management objectives. We therefore employed an expert panel to determine which of three alternative personnel management concepts best mitigated the risks and exploited the opportunities inherent in implementing RAF in the anticipated security environment. Informed by the panel results, we then estimated the number of billets requiring regional expertise that was implied by the alternative selected.

Modeling the Army's Ability to Develop and Maintain the Appropriate Personnel Inventory

Having established the approximate size of the requirement, the next step was to assess the Army's ability to meet it. To do so, we developed a simulation that analyzes soldiers' assignment history to assess the degree of regional depth and breadth that the force could have generated under a given alignment of forces and regions. The simulation assesses the number of different regions to which soldiers could have been assigned (breadth) and the extent to which they have served in the same region (depth) over the course of their careers. We compared outputs with the aforementioned estimates of requirements of regional expertise for select career management fields (CMFs), including infantry, engineers, field artillery, aviation, signal corps, military intelligence, and psychological operations.

Identifying Required Changes to Personnel Management Practices and Capabilities

The final step was to determine what changes to Army personnel management practices and capabilities might be required in order to match soldiers who have regional expertise to the billets that require it. We analyzed the actual and potential capabilities inherent in the current system and planned modifications. In particular, we considered how the Army's planned evolution to a talent management approach might affect the development of regional expertise across the force.

Findings

The Army Has Relatively Little Empirical Information About the Personnel Implications of Regionally Aligned Forces

The Army has been implementing RAF, on a very limited scale, since 2013. The 2nd Brigade Combat Team (BCT), 1st Infantry Division, was the first of this initial batch of RAF and has acquired significant experience in Africa. It is in this vein that we note that most actual deployments have occurred at brigade level and below. Perhaps more to the point is the fact that very few soldiers in tactical units have had extensive opportunities to acquire expertise about places besides Iraq and Afghanistan. Although there are some parallels between counterinsurgency operations in those two countries and the military engagement missions envisioned under RAF, the differences probably outweigh the similarities. At this point, there has been almost no opportunity to compare the ability of different approaches to manning the force to support RAF, let alone determine that one alternative is clearly superior to others.

Potential Demand for Regional Expertise Appears Likely to Be Moderate at This Time

To develop a solution, we must first understand the scope and scale of the problem. The limited feedback from tactical units available seems to indicate that functional expertise—such as command post operations, battalion tactics, or weapon handling—far outweighs regional expertise in importance and that predeployment training seems capable of providing the limited degree of regional knowledge required. Instead, our research indicates that demand for regional expertise might be concentrated at the operational level, at the division echelon and higher, and in theater-level enablers, particularly intelligence, logistics, and signal units. Initial estimates suggest that the eventual requirement might not exceed 4,300 soldiers, at least in an Army of approximately the same size and composition of today's Army. As with any other conclusion about the future direction of the RAF initiative, this finding rests on very limited empirical data. Our expert panel's collective experience in the kinds of operational environments envisioned under RAF is likewise limited. As the Army acquires additional experience with RAF, this estimate should be reviewed and might be subject to revision.

Acquiring Regional Expertise Need Not Conflict with Traditional Career Development Patterns

A key conclusion is that acquiring appropriate regional expertise need not conflict with normal career progression, at least not substantially. In past discussions of this issue, most stakeholders simply assumed that acquiring regional expertise could come only at the cost of functional experience. The Afghanistan–Pakistan (AFPAK) Hands concept is often seen as a potential model for personnel management under RAF because it has a similar objective: improving military forces' understanding of the dynamics of their operational environments. A widely shared perception is that service as an AFPAK Hand was detrimental to a soldier's career progression. Whether that perception is accurate, the analogy is inapt. The AFPAK Hands program assigned soldiers— and sailors, airmen, and marines—to nontraditional jobs outside of traditional career development tracks. To the extent that RAF might affect career management, however, it will do so by requiring soldiers to perform jobs already on their career tracks, albeit in particular regions.

The Army Will Probably Produce Enough Soldiers with Relevant Expertise to Meet This Modest Demand

The Army does not have an extensive inventory of soldiers with expertise in regions other than the U.S. Central Command (CENTCOM) AOR. It is thus necessary to estimate the future inventory of soldiers with different regional experience that might accumulate over time as the Army implements RAF. Our simulation suggests that the Army will likely accrue sufficient inventories of such personnel after several years of RAF implementation. Depending on the degree of experience required, the Army should be able to fill positions with regionally experienced personnel and still retain a modicum of selectivity.

Current Personnel Management Practices and Recordkeeping Systems Do Not Enable the Army to Match Supply with Demand

There are probably assignments that require a significant degree of regional expertise or for which a significant degree of such expertise would be extraordinarily useful; our simulation indicates that a sufficient number of soldiers probably have the needed expertise. The problem is that it is very hard to match the supply with the demand. For the most part, data about soldiers' regionally relevant experience, education, and training are available neither to assignment personnel nor to units in the field.

Recommendations

Leverage the Army's Adoption of Talent Management

Given the low level of experience with RAF and the concomitantly high level of uncertainty about what it requires, **the Army should incrementally adapt its personnel system to support RAF.** The Army should undertake mostly measures that promise benefits no matter what it learns from RAF implementation or at least minimize costs. For example, the Army should not remake its entire personnel system to support RAF based on the limited information available today.

On the other hand, the Army is adopting a personnel management approach of talent management, which can support RAF in addition to many other imperatives. Talent management is a broad and often ill-defined subject. In this context, it involves matching soldiers to positions based on the soldiers' unique competencies and the positions' specific requirements. It contrasts with the current military personnel system, which assigns soldiers based simply on CMF and grade.

Leveraging talent management would enable the Army to learn from experience which billets require what degree of regional expertise, rather than trying to guess correctly in advance. Commands and units could indicate the positions they believe require regional expertise and the degree of education and experience required. As mentioned earlier, most positions would probably require no significant amount of prior regional experience or education. Assignment officers and assignment managers could then nominate soldiers who best meet the various criteria—regional and otherwise—to fill those positions. By observing and analyzing this process over time, the Army could identify which positions require some degree of regional expertise; incorporate these requirements into appropriate objectives and assignment criteria; and adapt education, training, and career development models to provide soldiers with the required expertise more efficiently.

Make Soldiers' Regionally Aligned Forces–Relevant Education and Experience Available to Personnel Managers

A talent management approach requires relevant information to function effectively. As indicated earlier, Army personnel managers lack information about soldiers' RAF-relevant education and experience. We have focused on the issue of regionally relevant military experience, but soldiers' personal experience and education are also relevant. Thus, the Army should provide such information.

Personnel development skill identifiers (PDSIs) provide a ready-made vehicle for doing so. The Army already uses PDSIs to track certain key skills gained through experience or on-the-job training, such as digital training. PDSIs differ from other kinds of skill identifiers in that they track soldier attributes but do not constitute requirements that a soldier must meet in order to fill an individual billet. In other words, PDSIs provide information that is useful to but not binding on personnel managers. The Army could use PDSIs to track formal education, training, and experience related to particular regions and to convey that information to personnel managers at the Army and unit levels. Requesting units could use them to identify the kind and amount of education and experience desired for different positions.

Although PDSIs exist, they are largely invisible to personnel managers under the current system. The Soldier Record Brief (SRB), to be deployed under the Integrated Personnel and Pay System—Army, includes a field for PDSIs. **Although a soldier can acquire many PDSIs over the course of a career, the Army could prioritize RAF-relevant PDSIs for inclusion in this field on the SRB.**

Allow a Regional Qualification System to Evolve

In the course of this study, a panel of Army and RAND experts concluded that a regional qualification system, in which the Army would reserve certain key billets for soldiers with appropriate levels of regional expertise, would best mitigate risks and exploit opportunities inherent in personnel management in support of RAF implementation. The panel determined that the kind of positions that might require regional expertise existed mostly at operational echelons. Those echelons include joint task force (JTF)–capable division and corps headquarters and operational enablers, such as theater sustainment commands, theater intelligence brigades, and strategic signal brigades. Positions tentatively included staff principals, planners, and technical experts with theater-level responsibilities.

Neither the panel nor any other participant in this study had the opportunity to identify specific billets requiring such regional expertise in any sort of analytically rigorous fashion. Even if any of them had had such opportunity, none has much empirical experience on which to base such analysis. Attempting to identify specific billets in advance thus incurs significant risk of identifying the wrong ones.

Fortunately, it is unnecessary to do so. If soldiers' regional expertise does contribute significantly to success in certain billets, one would expect to observe the Army selecting soldiers with such expertise for such jobs at significantly higher rates than soldiers who lack such expertise under a talent management system. **Army personnel managers should thus analyze assignment decisions made in this context over time in order to determine which positions benefit from regional expertise and which do not.** Results might well differ depending on the region. Senior leaders should periodically review their analysis to ensure that personnel managers' assessments are consistent with those of the Army's needs.

Conclusion

The RAF concept affects the nature of the Army's operational demands and thus implies some change for the Army goals, objectives, and criteria that guide activities in the personnel system. The extremely limited empirical information available to date seems to point to some sort of regional qualification system, in which prior regional education and experience will serve as prerequisites for selection to certain key billets.

Our analysis indicates that the Army will probably develop enough soldiers with the requisite expertise to meet the demands that a regional qualification might impose, at least in an Army of approximately the same size and posture as today's Army. The problem lies in identifying the billets that require such expertise and matching the right soldiers to those billets. There is a risk, however, that attempting to identify billets and specific requirements based on information now available will lead to error later.

Talent management addresses the problem and its accompanying risk, allowing the Army's internal labor market to identify both the billets that require expertise and the nature of the expertise needed to fill them. The key to this approach is providing personnel managers with information about soldiers' RAF-relevant education and experience and enabling them to make decisions based on that information.

Acknowledgments

We would like to thank our sponsors, Anthony J. Stamilio and MG Thomas C. Seamands, for their support of this project and insights. We would also like to thank COL Tammy L. Miracle and MAJ Scott Johnson in the Office of the Deputy Assistant Secretary of the Army for Military Personnel and COL Cheryl Martinez, MAJ Marie Slack, and MAJ Adam Smith of the Directorate of Military Personnel Management for their oversight of our research. We would also like to thank the many military and civilian officials who responded to our inquiries, especially participants in our expert panel on the future evolution of the Army personnel system in support of Regionally Aligned Forces. Without their generous commitment of time and energy, this project would not have been possible.

We would also like to thank our reviewers, Michael J. Colarusso of the U.S. Army Office of Economic and Manpower Analysis and Michael J. McNerney of RAND, for their thoughtful reviews of this document. Finally, we owe a debt of thanks to Gina Frost for coordinating project meetings and shepherding this document through the RAND Arroyo Center publishing process.

Abbreviations

AC	Active Component
ACFLS	Army Culture and Foreign Language Strategy
ACOM	Army command
AFPAK	Afghanistan–Pakistan
AFRICOM	U.S. Africa Command
AOC	area of concentration
AOR	area of responsibility
APMS	assistant professor of military science
ASI	additional skill identifier
BCT	brigade combat team
BOLC	Basic Officer Leaders Course
CENTCOM	U.S. Central Command
CGSOC	Command and General Staff Officers' Course
CMF	career management field
COCOM	combatant command
CSA	chief of staff, Army
CTC	Combat Training Center
DA	Department of the Army
DoD	U.S. Department of Defense
FA	functional area

FAO	foreign area officer
G-1	U.S. Army Deputy Chief of Staff for Personnel
GRF	global response force
HRC	U.S. Army Human Resources Command
ID	infantry division
JIIM	joint, interagency, intergovernmental, or multinational
JP	joint publication
JTF	joint task force
KSA	knowledge, skill, or ability
KSAO	knowledge, skill, ability, or other characteristic
LREC	language, regional expertise, and culture
MOS	military occupational specialty
NATO	North Atlantic Treaty Organization
NCO	noncommissioned officer
O/C-T	observer/controller-trainer
OEMA	Office of Economic and Manpower Analysis
OJE	on-the-job experience
OJT	on-the-job training
PAM	pamphlet
PDSI	personnel development skill identifier
RAF	Regionally Aligned Forces
RC	Reserve Component
RCA	regional cadre alternative
RDA	regional depth alternative
RGR	ranger
ROTC	Reserve Officer Training Corps
S3	operations officer

SAMS	School of Advanced Military Studies
SMU	special mission unit
SOF	special operations forces
SOUTHCOM	U.S. Southern Command
SQI	special qualification identifier
SRB	Soldier Record Brief
TAPDB	Total Army Personnel Database
TRADOC	U.S. Army Training and Doctrine Command
UIC	unit identification code
USAJFKSWCS	U.S. Army John F. Kennedy Special Warfare Center and School
USAREUR	U.S. Army Europe
USARPAC	U.S. Army Pacific
USARSO	U.S. Army South
USMA	U.S. Military Academy
USPACOM	U.S. Pacific Command
VTIP	Voluntary Transfer Incentive Program
WO	warrant officer
XO	executive officer

CHAPTER ONE

Introduction

The Regionally Aligned Forces Concept

The Army is implementing the Regionally Aligned Forces (RAF) concept in order to better support combatant commanders in executing a strategy focusing on military engagement and conflict prevention. The RAF concept is intended to enhance relationships among Army, joint, and other relevant planning staffs at the regional level and to improve Army units' familiarity with and expertise regarding the geographic regions in which they are likely to be employed. For some time, U.S. declaratory strategy has emphasized the importance of preventing instability and conflict by engaging with allies and partners (see U.S. Department of Defense [DoD], 2008; Gates, 2010; U.S. Joint Chiefs of Staff, 2012b; Panetta, 2012; DoD, 2014a). As operations in Iraq and Afghanistan wind down, the Army can begin to shift its attention to supporting that strategy.

Although it notes the complexity and challenge of the emerging security environment, *Army Strategic Planning Guidance 2013* emphasizes the opportunities that environment presents to

> shape relationships with nonhostile rivals, avoiding conditions and misunderstandings that could escalate to war; work with friends, partners and allies to expand and encourage conditions of favorable order; and work with weaker states to manage unacceptable levels of disorder short of major combat operations or strategic strike options. (Odierno and McHugh, 2013, p. 3)

Regional alignment of forces is thus intended to improve Army forces' regional familiarity so that they can better "deter and counter the opportunists seeking to exploit instability and threaten American interests" (Odierno and McHugh, 2013, p. 3).

Implementing RAF effectively requires forces shaped for the specific operational environments to which they might be deployed. In a 2013 article for *Parameters*, then-BG Kimberly Field, then-COL James Learmont, and then-LTC Jason Charland wrote,

> Accomplishing such regional missions requires an understanding of the cultures, geography, languages, and militaries of the countries where RAF are most likely to

be employed, as well as expertise in how to impart military knowledge and skills to others. (Field, Learmont, and Charland, 2013, p. 56)[1]

The question animating this study is whether and how the Army should adapt its personnel management policies and practices to facilitate that understanding. Beyond competence in specific languages and culture, it is possible to imagine additional knowledge, skills, abilities, and other characteristics (KSAOs) that might be needed in particular regional contexts. However, the Army's ability to identify and track such KSAOs throughout soldiers' careers is limited and constrained. Regional alignment thus appears to have potential implications for leader development and personnel management, but the magnitude and direction of these implications have yet to be identified.

Research Objective

Accordingly, the Assistant Secretary of the Army for Manpower and Reserve Affairs and the U.S. Army Deputy Chief of Staff for Personnel (G-1) asked the RAND Arroyo Center to help the Army adapt its personnel and manpower management systems to support the RAF concept while continuing to develop leaders' capabilities to conduct unified land operations worldwide. Later in this chapter, we explain our approach for meeting this objective. First, we offer some background on the Army personnel management system.

The Army Personnel Management System

To understand RAF's implications for Army personnel management policies and practices, we must understand the current state of the Army personnel management system. That system is not designed to foster the development of regional expertise in the conventional force. Instead, the objective of that system is to develop soldiers with the right mix of *functional* breadth and depth in their career management fields (CMFs) to man operational Army units and supporting organizations in the institutional Army.[2]

---

[1]   Field was, at the time, deputy director of Strategy, Plans and Policy in the Office of the Deputy Chief of Staff, G-3/5/7. Learmont led the Stability Support Division of the Strategy, Plans and Policy Directorate of the Office of the Deputy Chief of Staff, G-3/5/7, and Charland was lead strategist for that division.

[2]   This discussion summarizes information found in Department of the Army (DA) Pamphlets (PAMs) 600-3 (U.S. Army, 2014b) and 600-25 (U.S. Army, 2008).

The system itself consists of four basic elements:

- education and training
- experience in key and developmental assignments to hone skills acquired in training and education
- selection and promotion of the most qualified for positions of greater responsibility
- a management framework integrating education, experience, and selection.

Education and training are focused on soldiers' functional specialties: Initial entry training focuses on military skills common to every CMF, while subsequent skill training emphasizes skills unique to particular CMFs. Throughout their careers, soldiers have the opportunity to acquire language and cultural skills during unit training, professional education, and self-development. However, except for career linguists and a few other select CMFs, such skills are neither required nor tracked systematically.[3]

As with education and training, Army career development models emphasize functional proficiency. Figure 1.1 illustrates that emphasis clearly. The chart depicts infantry officers' career progression, including both key and developmental positions in command and staff assignments, as well as optional developmental opportunities, such as graduate education and other broadening assignments. These opportunities are described in functional terms; no mention is made either of regional education or experience, though opportunities to obtain and broaden regional expertise clearly exist. A similar pattern exists with regard to warrant officers (WOs) and enlisted soldiers.

The Army incentivizes soldiers' acquisition of knowledge, skills, and abilities (KSAs) through its promotion and selection policies and practices. These policies and practices also emphasize functional competencies. A soldier's eligibility for promotion and selection is tied to completion of key and developmental assignments, which are defined in terms of function, not region. For example, service as an operations officer or executive officer (XO)—or an analogous position—at the battalion echelon or higher is virtually a prerequisite for an infantry major's promotion to lieutenant colonel; service in any particular region of the world is not. To the extent that regional alignment affects promotion opportunities, such influence is incidental to operational service. Combat or other operational experience is a marked advantage in terms of selection and promotion; such experience is inextricably attached to a particular country or region.

The RAF brings a new concept to Army's force management, with possible implications for its personnel and manpower management systems. To implement RAF, virtually every operational Army unit not already aligned with the global response force

---

[3] Soldiers can have their language proficiency evaluated and noted in their records voluntarily. However, officials indicate that many do not do so.

Figure 1.1
Active Component Infantry (Area of Concentration 11A) Career Development Model

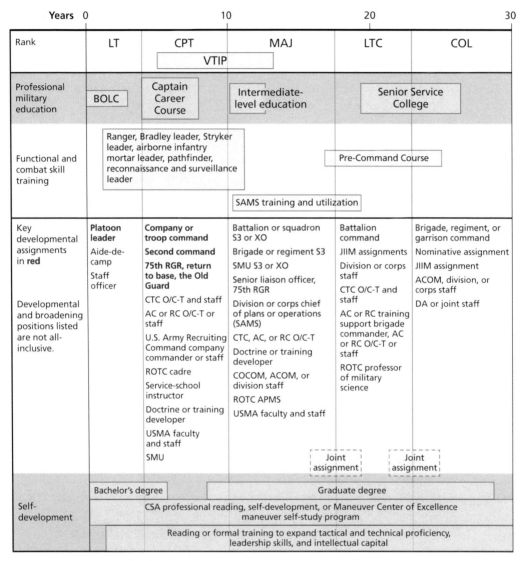

SOURCE: U.S. Army, 2014b, Figure 8.1.
NOTE: VTIP = Voluntary Transfer Incentive Program. BOLC = Basic Officer Leaders Course. SAMS = School of Advanced Military Studies. RGR = ranger. CTC = Combat Training Center. O/C-T = observer/controller-trainer. AC = Active Component. RC = Reserve Component. COCOM = combatant command. ROTC = Reserve Officer Training Corps. APMS = assistant professor of military science. USMA = U.S. Military Academy. SMU = special mission unit. S3 = operations officer. ACOM = Army command. JIIM = joint, interagency, intergovernmental, or multinational. CSA = chief of staff, Army.
RAND RR1065-1.1

(GRF) will be assigned, allocated, or otherwise aligned with a geographic combatant command and adapt its training and other preparations to the particular requirements of the region with which it is aligned. Corps and division headquarters are to be aligned with regions for periods exceeding one Army Force Generation cycle. The alignment of echelons below division, however, will probably have to shift with demand and cannot be expected to last more than one 24-month readiness cycle (Field, Learmont, and Charland, 2013). Under RAF, forces can be assigned to geographic combatant commands, allocated for planning purposes, or retained by the Army and prepared for operations with a specific combatant command. The last status is formally referred to as service-retained combatant command–aligned.

Research Approach

We used a three-pronged approach to examine the implications of RAF for the Army's personnel management practices and policies:

- First, we estimated the potential scope and scale of the requirements for regional expertise.
- Next, we modeled the Army's ability to produce soldiers with the required expertise under normal assignment policies and practices.
- Finally, we identified low-cost, low-regret modifications to the personnel management system required to match soldiers who possess the desired level of expertise with the positions requiring it.

We discuss these ideas in more detail in this section.

The concept of *expertise* underpins this study. Note that our use of the term *expertise* does not indicate that we think that soldiers need to become experts in a particular region. Rather, we use the term *regional expertise* to connote *the combination of formal education and developmental experiences that enables effective performance in a particular regional context.* Such expertise can take many forms and be gained through many combinations of education and experience.

Although language and cultural proficiency are important components of regional expertise, it would be a mistake to simply equate the latter with the former. For some positions, such understanding might indeed prove critical. For others, an intuitive understanding of the possibilities and constraints that the region's military geography imposes on operational maneuver might be even more important. For example, French commanders attributed the success of their 2013 intervention in Mali in large part to their understanding of how such factors constrained friendly and enemy options. The planning and conduct of operational logistics was particularly important (Mirikelam, 2014). In a European context, understanding of North Atlantic Treaty Organization (NATO) doctrine and staff processes is far more important to officials from NATO partners than understanding their local culture (Markel et al., 2011). In short, the regional context matters, but it matters in different ways, in different regions, for different positions.

Soldiers can develop the necessary level of expertise through any number of combinations of education and experience. They might acquire the requisite education in military or civilian institutions, before or after they join the Army. They might obtain the necessary education through research and writing. Experience could come as a function of military deployments, through travel abroad, or as a result of family background. The Army can acquire needed expertise through new accessions, such as the interpreter/translator program or the Military Accessions Vital to the National Interest program (U.S. Army, undated [a]; DoD, 2014b).

As the term *regional expertise* suggests, we *assume* that regions have distinctive characteristics that are common across many, if not most, of the countries that make up the region. For the purpose of this analysis, we assume that regions are more or less equivalent to combatant commands' areas of responsibility (AORs). Clearly, there are divisions within regions as well as across regions. Sub-Saharan Africa presents a significantly different set of challenges from those of North Africa. In spite of Africa's many indigenous languages and dialects, English and French are widely spoken. Within the U.S. Pacific Command (USPACOM) AOR, India differs significantly from other countries, such as Japan and the Republic of Korea, and both differ from archipelagos, such as the Philippines and Indonesia. Still, there are commonalities. Nations in the USPACOM AOR might differ in many respects, but they share a concern with China's growing power and assertiveness. It might well be, however, that the only relevant expertise concerns individual countries in which U.S. forces might operate. Preparing soldiers with militarily relevant expertise about the unique characteristics of a full range of countries in a region, however, is probably infeasible. For the moment, we are content to operate on the assumption that regional, as opposed to country-specific, expertise is both useful and possible to obtain.

According to the academic literature on the subject, experience plays the dominant role in the development of expertise (see Ericsson, Krampe, and Tesch-Römer, 1993; Ericsson, 2006; Lord and Maher, 1991; Bransford, Brown, and Cocking, 1998; Klein, 1999; Norman et al., 2006). The ten-year and 10,000-hour rules are frequently cited, though neither estimate is precise. Without an opportunity to practice one's discipline in a relevant context, either real or simulated in training, expertise is necessarily degraded. Of course, it might not be possible for soldiers to obtain meaningful experience with regard to the conduct of military operations—including military engagement—in certain countries. In such cases, formal education becomes particularly important.

Although we acknowledge the potential importance of education and training, this study does not explore further requirements for them. An internal Army study, conducted in parallel with this one, was already doing so, and we did not wish to duplicate its efforts. Our analysis therefore assumes that the Army will correctly identify education requirements and develop effective programs of instruction for meeting them. Instead, our study focuses on the problem of ensuring that graduates of such programs are utilized effectively. The major issue this study confronts is managing soldiers' assignments to ensure that the Army develops the appropriate reservoirs of regional expertise.

Estimating the Potential Scope and Scale of Personnel Requirements

The Army personnel management system supports Army operational capabilities by providing soldiers with the appropriate expertise for the positions they must fill. Our first step was therefore to establish how many billets, of which grades, and of which CMFs might be affected by the need to better support RAF. To do so, we followed a three-step process. First, we interviewed stakeholders at various echelons in the operational Army and the Army's personnel management community in order to identify potential risks and opportunities inherent in implementing RAF under the current personnel management system or plausible alternative concepts. Next, we convened an expert panel to assess which of those alternatives would best mitigate those risks. Finally, we identified potential billets that, based on the panel's assessment, might require regional expertise.

The expert panel considered three alternative concepts, which differed with respect to degree of expertise deemed necessary to function effectively in the RAF concept and the scale of the requirement, defined in terms of the kinds of billets for which regional expertise was deemed necessary. The alternatives included

- the **current personnel system**, which prioritizes the development of functional expertise
- a **regional qualification system**, in which key billets at operational and strategic echelons would be designated for fill by soldiers with appropriate levels of regional expertise
- a **regional depth alternative (RDA)**, in which most soldiers would be aligned with a particular region throughout most of their careers.

Modeling the Army's Ability to Develop and Maintain the Appropriate Personnel Inventory

Once we established the approximate size of the requirement, the next step was to assess the Army's ability to meet it. To do so, the research team developed a simulation that analyzes soldiers' assignment history to assess the degree of regional depth and breadth that the force could have generated under a given alignment of forces and regions. *Breadth* refers to the number of different regions to which soldiers could have been assigned over the course of their careers, while *depth* refers to the extent to which they have served in the same region. We compared outputs with the estimates of requirements of regional expertise for select CMFs.

We stress repeatedly that the results are only a simulation of what the Army could do over the course of several years, given certain patterns of regional alignment. To the extent that current soldiers are regionally aligned, it is probably with the U.S. Central Command (CENTCOM) AOR—specifically, Iraq and Afghanistan. Therefore, it will take several years before the Army can begin to significantly expand its reservoir of regional expertise with respect to other combatant commands' AORs.

Identifying Required Changes to Personnel Management Practices and Capabilities

The final step was to determine what changes to Army personnel management practices and capabilities might be required in order to match soldiers with regional expertise to the billets that require it. We analyzed the actual and potential capabilities inherent in the current system along with planned modifications. In particular, we considered how the Army's planned evolution to a talent management approach might affect the development of regional expertise across the force. Such an approach would involve matching soldiers to positions based on the soldiers' unique competencies and the positions' specific requirements.

Organization of This Report

The remainder of this report is organized into five chapters and an appendix:

- Chapter Two describes the current state of RAF implementation, including an overview of significant professional educational and institutional training opportunities that can contribute to the development of regional expertise.
- Chapter Three presents our estimate of the potential requirement for regional expertise and explains the basis on which it rests.
- Chapter Four explains our assessment of the Army's ability to meet the requirement described in Chapter Three.
- Chapter Five assesses the changes needed to the Army personnel management system to enable the Army to match the supply of soldiers possessing relevant regional expertise with the demand for them.
- Chapter Six summarizes our findings and recommendations.
- The appendix presents the methods, analysis, and results of the expert panel elicitations.

CHAPTER TWO

The Current State of Regionally Aligned Forces Implementation

As a broad concept, RAF is clear, simple, and fairly well understood: Every Army unit, except for forces assigned to the GRF, is to be aligned with a geographic combatant command. Such alignment is supposed to improve the Army's ability to support combatant commanders, which is one of the reasons such alignment was required even before 9/11 (U.S. Joint Chiefs of Staff, 2002). The tangible implications of that concept are not necessarily obvious, however, leading one commentator to write, "The service's plan [RAF] to revamp itself for the post-post-9/11 world is ambiguous and rife with contradiction. That's what makes it brilliant" (R. Brooks, 2014, p. 43). Because of the uncertainty surrounding RAF, it is important to review what is known about RAF's implementation to date.

In this chapter, we describe the kinds of missions conducted under RAF's aegis and review the capabilities used to prepare units for those missions. We also assess the degree to which the Army's recent experience in counterinsurgency operations might offer insights into their intended employment under RAF. Finally, we consider the range of institutional training and education opportunities focused on preparing soldiers for service in particular regions.

As we show in this chapter, the analysis indicates that there is relatively little in the way of empirical evidence from which to derive a clear path forward for supporting RAF. Relatively few Army forces have actually accrued operational experience under RAF. Such experience is mostly at the tactical level. The nature of that experience has differed substantially in each region, not just in terms of geography but also in terms of the nature of operations undertaken. Parallels exist between forces' employment envisioned under RAF and experience in overseas contingency operations, but the differences are at least as great as the similarities. Experience thus offers only meager indications about future directions for the Army personnel system.

The Army's Experience with Regionally Aligned Forces to Date

The CSA first used the term *Regionally Aligned Forces* in a speech in October 2012 (Field, Learmont, and Charland, 2013). The Army began implementing RAF in the spring of 2013, with the deployment of elements of the 2nd Brigade Combat Team (BCT), 1st Infantry Division (ID), to Africa. By the time of this writing, elements of up to four of the Army's 38 AC BCTs, with associated enablers, had deployed under RAF (Allyn et al., 2013; McHugh and Odierno, 2014). Elements of one of the Army National Guard's 28 BCTs also deployed to South America. Most RAF activities have been tactical in nature, focused on imparting specific skills to partners or the conduct of a particular exercise. There has been far less engagement at the division and corps levels. The rest of this section describes the nature of those deployments in each combatant command's AOR.

U.S. Africa Command

In the early spring of 2013, elements of the Army's 2nd BCT, 1st ID, deployed to Africa as a proof of concept. The division's mission involved mostly training partners' military forces (U.S. Army Africa, 2013). Although the BCT includes about 3,800 soldiers, no single deployment exceeded 5 percent of the overall total. Missions involved as few as two soldiers on the ground for a brief period of time, or up to several hundred to participate in a joint exercise (Tan, 2013b; McHugh and Odierno, 2014).

The division's preparations for deployments focused on these missions. The brigade established a training capability it called "Dagger U" to facilitate language, region, and culture training for teams deploying to various African nations. The brigade coordinated support from Kansas State University, including instruction from exchange students from the region on conditions in their home countries. These teams also completed training with U.S. Army Forces Command's 162nd Infantry Brigade, which trained forces for the advisory mission (Field, Learmont, and Charland, 2013).

U.S. Central Command

Elements of the 1st Armored Division were also deployed to Kuwait as part of RAF. As with 2nd BCT, 1st ID, the division focused on building partner capacity. That focus took a significantly different form, however, in that most such engagements took the form of joint exercises, staff talks, or demonstrations. The division participated in several joint exercises with Jordan and other Middle Eastern allies of the United States (Grigsby et al., 2013).

U.S. European Command

The 1st BCT, 1st Cavalry Division, deployed elements to take part in joint exercises as part of the NATO Response Force in May 2014. Later that year, other elements also deployed to the Baltic states as part of Operation Atlantic Resolve, an effort to reassure NATO allies in the face of Russian adventurism in Ukraine (McHugh and Odierno, 2014; DoD, undated; U.S. European Command, 2014). In contrast to RAF deployments in the U.S. Africa Command (AFRICOM) and CENTCOM AORs, which focused on building partners' capacity, these efforts focus on conventional warfighting under a NATO umbrella (U.S. Army Europe [USAREUR], 2014). Preparations for these deployments reflected this focus.

U.S. Pacific Command

U.S. Army Pacific's (USARPAC's) primary vehicle for engagement under the RAF concept is the Pacific Pathways program. That program involves a series of joint exercises with partner nations. Beginning in the fall of 2014, the 3rd Stryker BCT, 2nd ID, began its cycle. USARPAC focuses on enhancing interoperability and building relationships with partners' military forces and defense officials through joint exercises and the associated coordination (Olsen, 2014a, 2014b; Truesdell, 2014).

U.S. Southern Command

In the late spring of 2014, the Georgia National Guard's 48th BCT became the first Army BCT to execute missions in U.S. Southern Command (SOUTHCOM) under RAF's aegis. Small teams from this unit are currently engaged in El Salvador, Honduras, and Guatemala in support of SOUTHCOM's initiatives to counter drugs and limit transnational organized crime. Primary activities include building partners' capacity in such areas as basic marksmanship, command and control, border security, and intelligence operations (SOUTHCOM officials, 2014; U.S. Army South [USARSO] official 1, 2014).

Overall Findings About the Army's Experience with Regionally Aligned Forces

The Army has been implementing RAF only for a short time, with the first RAF unit in 2013, while the Pacific Pathways program started in the fall of 2014. Relatively few forces have been involved—about four of the Army's 38 BCTs and a few associated enablers. The nature of the missions that RAF forces conducted in each AOR varies substantially, as did RAF units' preparations for those missions. The success of these approaches remains to be formally assessed.

The evidence points to two major conclusions:

- First, this limited experience does not provide a clear direction for adapting the Army to support RAF. It remains too soon to tell.
- Second, the variation in missions and preparation for each theater indicates that RAF's implications for Army personnel management are likely to differ for each theater as well.

Other Sources of Experience

The Army has also accrued RAF-relevant experience outside of the RAF context. For example, the Army has been integrating its capabilities with those of partners in Europe and Korea for more than 60 years. Army forces have acquired considerable experience in multinational operations and building partners' capacity in counterinsurgency operations in Iraq and Afghanistan as well. To a limited extent, those experiences offer some insight for personnel management in support of RAF.

The RAF concept departs from historical precedent in that it envisions the widespread employment of Army conventional forces for military engagement and security cooperation.[1] In more-concrete terms, military engagement and security cooperation typically involve activities to train, advise, and assist partner nations' security forces in building their capabilities; civil military operations to foster goodwill; and combined exercises to enhance interoperability. Traditionally, such operations have been the province of special operations forces (SOF), especially Army special forces, civil affairs, and psychological operations units.

Certainly, Army conventional forces have engaged extensively in developing Iraqi and Afghan security forces, but such activities have taken place within a robust supporting infrastructure, such as the NATO Training Mission—Afghanistan or the Multi-National Security Transition Command—Iraq. Moreover, these activities have usually been secondary to combat operations. Under RAF, conventional forces are likely to be primarily focused on military engagement rather than combat and operate with less supporting infrastructure (Field, Learmont, and Charland, 2013). In short, RAF envisions different forces operating in different manners in significantly different operational environments, a situation very different from what has been the case recently.

Army Capabilities for Enhancing Regional Expertise

The Army has a range of capabilities for enhancing soldiers' language, regional, and cultural skills, many of which we describe in this section. At the current time, however, these capabilities are neither tracked nor required for assignment to organizations aligned with a particular region. The capabilities described are available mostly to officers.

---

[1]   Joint Publication (JP) 1-02, 2012, defines military engagement as

> Routine contact and interaction between individuals or elements of the Armed Forces of the United States and those of another nation's armed forces, or foreign and domestic civilian authorities or agencies to build trust and confidence, share information, coordinate mutual activities, and maintain influence.

Security cooperation is defined as

> All Department of Defense interactions with foreign defense establishments to build defense relationships that promote specific US security interests, develop allied and friendly military capabilities for self-defense and multinational operations, and provide US forces with peacetime and contingency access to a host nation.

Cadet Education

All students at the USMA are required to take at least two semesters of a foreign language. Up to 150 cadets have the opportunity to study abroad for a semester, and up to 60 international cadets are fully integrated into cadet life at the academy (USMA, undated [a], undated [b]). Among ROTC cadets, the Cultural Understanding and Language Proficiency program encourages cadets to complete approved language and culture courses through the Culture and Language Incentive Pay-Bonus (U.S. Army Cadet Command, undated). Cultural Understanding and Language Proficiency offers a variety of other scholarship and study abroad programs, but its premier event is a three-week program for cadets to receive immersion training in one of 40 foreign countries. In 2013, around 1,200 cadets participated in this program (Project GO, undated).

Company-Grade Officer Education

Efforts are under way to better integrate language and culture into the program of instruction for officers at the U.S. Army Maneuver Center of Excellence. As of the summer of 2013, such efforts were focusing on identifying what should be integrated and determining how best to integrate it (McMaster, 2013).

Intermediate-Level Education

The Command and General Staff Officers' Course (CGSOC) provides a standardized program of language, regional expertise, and culture (LREC) instruction to all its resident students. CGSOC has a fairly robust formal program of LREC offerings, as well as informal exposure to foreign students who are attending the course and intimately involved in each seminar group. Every student takes a Culture 101 course as part of the core curriculum. Each student must also take at least one elective on an approved regional or cultural topic. LREC issues are integrated into the program of instruction in other ways. For example, planning exercises include cultural considerations in mission analysis. Foreign students also educate U.S. peers on their home countries. Many of these capabilities are unavailable to nonresident students, however (U.S. Army official, 2014).

Senior Service College

LREC courses do not constitute a formal requirement for graduation from the U.S. Army War College like they do at CGSOC. On the other hand, education of officers at that level is inherently focused on interagency and international issues. Courses in cultural awareness or offerings on culture and strategy illustrate this dynamic. The school's Department of Distance Education also offers courses in such topics as regional issues and interests and strategic leadership in a global environment (U.S. Army War College, undated).

U.S. Army Training and Doctrine Command Culture Center

The U.S. Army Training and Doctrine Command (TRADOC) Culture Center is the Army's lead activity for imparting cultural training to deploying units. It

> provides a relevant and accredited cultural competency training and education to soldiers and DA Civilians in order to build and sustain an Army with the right blend of cultural competency capabilities to facilitate a wide range of operations, now and in the future. (U.S. Army Combined Arms Center, 2015)

The TRADOC Culture Center provides this training principally through the use of mobile training teams, but it also develops distance-learning products for unit use.

Joint Base Lewis-McChord Language and Culture Center

Joint Base Lewis-McChord has created its own Language and Culture Center to enhance soldiers' language and cultural skills. Its purpose is to sustain specialists' language and culture skills and to provide initial training for others as part of preparations for employment, over and above training and education provided in other venues. For example, it seeks to increase key leaders' language proficiency to an elementary level, rather than the "memorized proficiency" level currently prescribed by DoD policy guidance (Joint Base Lewis-McChord Language and Culture Center, 2014).

Implications

The foregoing examples illustrate some of the many capabilities that the Army has developed to enhance soldiers' regional and cultural proficiency. The list is by no means exhaustive, but these and other educational opportunities can begin to serve as the educational components of regional expertise. For that to happen, however, regionally relevant education and training must be followed by operational experience in the region. With the exception of language proficiency, completion of these courses is not tracked in soldiers' personnel records. For example, although CGSOC resident students are required to complete some regional education requirements, their regional orientation appears nowhere on their Officer Record Brief. For all intents and purposes, such information is invisible to personnel managers. Soldiers' language proficiency can be part of their records. However, soldiers are not always keen to have such information available to assignment managers.[2]

---

[2]   Quite simply, soldiers with high-demand language skills can find themselves with repetitive assignments to unpleasant places. A soldier with good Dari or Pashto skills, for example, could find herself spending every other year in primitive parts of Afghanistan. Adding injury to insult is the fact that such assignments can come at the expense of more career-enhancing billets. For example, having a linguistically adept protocol officer might be very important to a local commander, but service in that billet is not nearly as impressive as service as an observer/controller.

Conclusion

RAF implementation remains in its infancy. Only a small fraction of the Army has deployed under RAF's aegis. Units deploying under RAF have conducted missions that differed substantially depending on the theater, mostly at the tactical level of war. Thus, it is premature to conclude, on the basis of such limited experience, what does or does not work.

Similarly, the Army has a range of capabilities for enhancing soldiers' capabilities for language and culture but has yet to integrate them into any program for developing specific regional expertise. Although the Army's previous experience is relevant to analysis about its future course, the range of operations envisioned under RAF differs enough from historical precedents to recommend caution about drawing conclusions from that experience.

CHAPTER THREE

Assessing Potential Requirements for Regional Expertise

To ascertain how the Army might need to adapt its personnel system to provide soldiers with appropriate regional expertise to support RAF implementation, we must assess the scope and scale of the requirement. In this context, *scope* refers to the types of position for which such expertise is required, while *scale* refers to the number of such positions. The type and number of billets requiring regional expertise will constrain the Army's options for filling them.

We followed a two-step process to assess the scope and scale of potential Army requirements for regional expertise. First, we identified a personnel management approach that best mitigated the risks and exploited the opportunities inherent in implementing RAF in the anticipated security environment. To do so, we convened a panel of Army and RAND subject-matter experts, complementing their findings with interviews with practitioners in the field. We describe the panel's results in this chapter and its methodology and results in greater detail in the appendix. Second, we assessed the concept's implications for the number and type of billets that would be required to support RAF implementation.

To preview the results, the expert panel determined that a regional cadre alternative (RCA) was the best approach to enhancing Army forces' capabilities for regional missions while minimizing the disruption to the Army personnel management system. Under the RCA, the Army would designate key billets in headquarters at the division level and above and in operational enablers (such as intelligence, signal, and logistics units) for fill by soldiers with regional expertise. Again, regional expertise consists of an appropriate combination of formal education and developmental experiences relevant to the region. Figure 3.1 depicts the implications of the RCA for Army requirements for regional expertise by grade and region. In the remainder of this chapter, we describe in more detail how we obtained these results and discuss their implications further.

Figure 3.1
Preliminary Estimate of Billets Requiring Regional Expertise

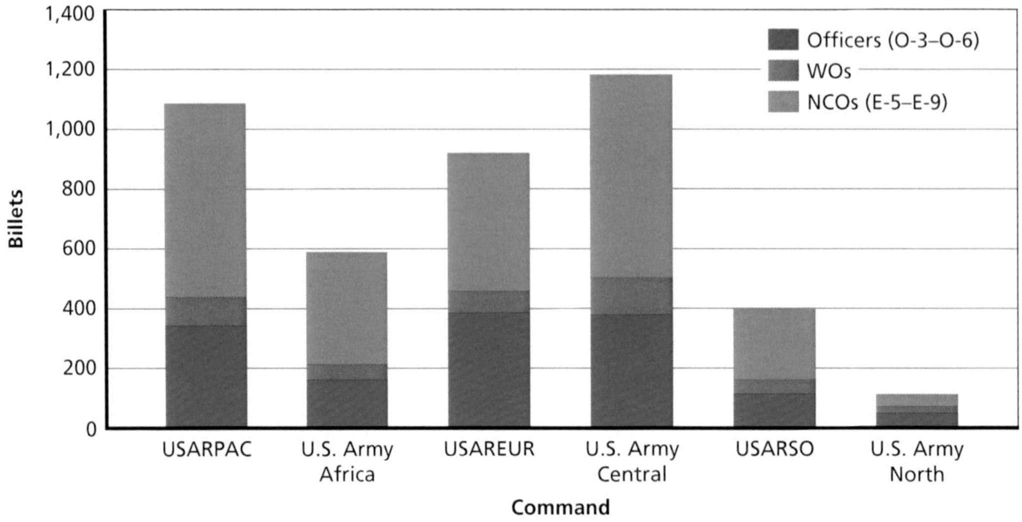

SOURCE: Our analysis of authorization documents.
NOTE: NCO = noncommissioned officer.
RAND *RR1065-3.1*

Identifying a Better Approach to Personnel Management to Support Implementation of Regionally Aligned Forces

In this section, we describe the composition of the expert panel, the alternatives that the panel considered, and the risks weighed. In the appendix, we describe the panel's organization, conduct, and especially the quantitative analysis of the results.

Respondent Characteristics

We selected the panel so as to balance operational and personnel management perspectives. The panel consisted of 12 participants,[1] drawn equally from the Army and the RAND Corporation. Army participants averaged 27 years of service and 31 months deployed during recent overseas contingency operations. Army and RAND groups were divided evenly between experts on personnel management and those with experience in conducting—or analyzing—recent operations similar to those envisioned under RAF. Army participants from the human resource community represented the Army G-1, U.S. Army Human Resources Command (HRC), and the U.S. Joint Chiefs of Staff Manpower and Personnel Directorate. All had extensive experience in person-

---

[1]   A representative from the sponsoring organization also participated, but we excluded his assessments from the analysis.

nel management. Army participants representing the operational perspective included a representative from I Corps and senior staff officers with extensive operational experience. There was considerable overlap between the operational and personnel management perspectives, particularly in the Army group. Soldiers representing the personnel management community had extensive operational experience, while several of those representing the operational perspective had served as personnel managers at one point or another during their career.

Alternatives Considered

The panel assessed three distinct alternative personnel management concepts:

- the **current personnel system**, which served as the analytic baseline. As noted in the introduction, this system emphasizes *functional* depth and, to a lesser extent, functional breadth. Overall, the current system does not develop, track, or utilize regional expertise explicitly in making assignment decisions. Except for designated experts, soldiers receive most regionally oriented training as a brief part of their pre-mission training.
- a regional depth alternative (**RDA**). Under this system, each soldier would be aligned with one particular region throughout the career. As one panel member observed, those careers are often quite short, with about 70 percent of first-term soldiers departing after their initial obligations. Nonetheless, the scope of this potential requirement would include most commissioned-officer, WO, and NCO positions in operational Army units, with the GRF serving as the exception. The scale would be immense. According to the Army's Force Management System, approximately 150,000 such positions are authorized to operational Army units. In short, in this alternative, almost every career soldier would develop depth in a particular region.
- a regional cadre alternative (**RCA**). This approach would designate key positions at the division level and higher—including operational-level enablers—for fill by soldiers with the appropriate education and prior experience in the region. The division level is significant because the division might be called on to provide the nucleus of a joint task force (JTF) in some regions. Critical operational enablers included military intelligence, signal, and logistics organizations that provided theater infrastructure.[2] The RCA differs from the RDA chiefly in the potential scale of the requirement. In the RDA, nearly everyone would need to acquire

---

[2] We developed this option based on interviews with selected practitioners. Their view was that military intelligence, signal, and logistics formations were most likely to be affected by distinctive regional characteristics. By definition, intelligence collection and analysis must enable commanders to understand the unique aspects of their operational environments. Operational logistics will be shaped by the geographic characteristics of the region and the commercial supply and distribution networks therein, while U.S. use of the electromagnetic spectrum will be constrained by host nations' rules and regulations on spectrum management.

regional depth. Under the RCA, the Army would need to produce only a relatively small number of soldiers to fill key billets. As we show later, there would probably be fewer than 5,000 such positions. Under this alternative, the soldiers filling these key positions would need to have acquired some degree of depth in a particular region. The concept is agnostic as to how they would do so.

Objectives for the Personnel Management System

To identify the personnel management concept best suited to providing soldiers with the right mix of functional and regional expertise to support RAF, the expert panel analyzed the potential of various options to mitigate the risks inherent in implementing RAF in the anticipated security environment. We identified eight overarching objectives for the Army's personnel management system based on information gleaned from interviews with stakeholders. Objectives fell into two broad categories: (1) support to operations generally and (2) personnel management. We asked panel members to weigh the extent to which improving performance with respect to one objective might present additional risks with respect to others.

Operational Objectives

Operational objectives described areas in which the degree of functional and regional expertise present could affect Army forces' ability to execute certain missions. Examples of operational objectives include the following:

- **regional security cooperation.** Participants assessed the degree to which alternative personnel management concepts could affect Army forces' ability to succeed in security cooperation activities conducted in regions with which units are aligned. Alternative personnel management concepts might enable Army forces to achieve greater or lesser effectiveness in training, advising, and assisting partners' forces because of soldiers' superior cultural understanding. Alternative concepts might also affect the degree to which soldiers develop personal relationships that could facilitate coordination with and access to potential partners.
- **regional contingency operations.** Participants evaluated alternative personnel management systems' effects on Army units' probability of mission success in contingency operations in the regions with which those forces are aligned. Contingency operations include the full range of military operations, from humanitarian assistance to major combat operations. Examples could include more-efficient noncombatant evacuation operations because of greater familiarity with the terrain or less-effective support to host-nation counterinsurgency efforts because of unfamiliarity with the operational environments in question.
- **global contingency operations.** This objective focuses on major contingency operations whose demands exceed the capacity of forces originally aligned with a particular region, requiring employment of forces aligned with other regions. For this category, participants assessed how well different personnel management

concepts support the employment of Army forces in regions with which they are not aligned and are therefore unfamiliar. Such operations include the full range of military operations but will probably consist of counterinsurgency or major combat operations. Examples include operations in which forces must deploy away from their regional orientations, such as when brigades from Korea were deployed to Iraq.

- **meeting combatant commanders' operational needs.** Participants also assessed the degree to which any posited improvement or degradation of soldiers' level of regional capability might increase or decrease the degree to which those forces meet combatant commands' operational needs. For example, it is theoretically possible, if combatant commands have little need for Army regional capabilities, that even a substantial improvement in Army forces' levels of regional capability might result in only very minor increases in demand.

Personnel Management Objectives

The panel also assessed alternative concepts' potential to complicate or enhance the Army's ability to achieve desired personnel management objectives. We identified four subcategories of personnel management risks:

- **cost.** Participants assessed alternatives' propensity to increase or decrease the costs associated with personnel management. Note that costs can include the costs of the personnel and technology to manage the system, the costs of any additional training and education provided to soldiers under the concept in question, or the costs of an enlarged trainees, transients, holdees, and students (that is, soldiers not assigned to units) account necessary to enable the Army to both man its formations and provide additional training. Costs can also be indirect and include the additional costs to unit training imposed by any personnel turbulence incurred by a particular personnel management concept.
- **other Army personnel management priorities.** Alternatives could also increase or decrease the Army's ability to achieve other priorities. Examples of such priorities include the acquisition of broadening experiences, enhancement of soldiers' adaptability, or management of soldiers' deployment tempos.
- **equity in assignment, selection, and promotion.** We asked participants to weigh the ability of alternative concepts to afford soldiers with an equitable opportunity to obtain desirable assignments, be selected for career-enhancing assignments, and be promoted to higher ranks. For example, it has been argued that soldiers assigned to a lower-priority region under the regional depth concept might be at risk for future promotion.
- **recruiting and retention.** Participants also considered how the dynamics of different personnel management systems might affect soldiers' perceptions of the desirability of an Army career. Enhanced education and training opportunities might increase the Army's ability to recruit and retain some soldiers while, for

others, alignment with an undesirable region might degrade the attractiveness of an Army career.

Results: The Expert Panel Preferred the Regional Cadre Alternative

Participants then assessed the alternatives relative to one another. First, they evaluated how well the baseline was likely to perform relative to the eight objectives. Next, they assessed the probability that alternatives would perform better than the current system with respect to each objective, perform significantly worse, or perform about the same. Participants also assessed the relative importance of each objective. We then computed an expected value for each alternative based on participants' ratings. The panel conducted two rounds of assessment, in between which participants discussed their rationales for their assessments.

Figure 3.2 depicts the results of their assessment. Each cluster of columns represents panelists' collective assessment of a particular alternative, with the red columns indicating the results of the first round and the blue columns indicating the results of the second. The error bar at the top of each column indicates the degree of convergence among panel members' assessments for that round.

As indicated by Figure 3.2, panelists consistently preferred the RCA to the other two alternatives. Indeed, its first-round score exceeded the best scores for either the current system (the analytic baseline) or the RDA. It is also significant to note that respondents felt after the second round that either alternative would perform better

Figure 3.2
Panelists' Assessment of Alternative Personnel Management Approaches: Overall Expected Value of Each Alternative Assessed

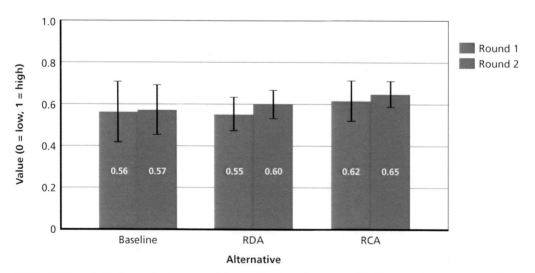

NOTE: Red bars indicate results from round 1, and blue bars from round 2. The error bar at the top of each column indicates the degree of convergence among panel members' assessments in that round.

than the baseline. Note also that this method did not allow respondents to assess *how much better* one alternative would perform for a specific objective. Instead, the assessment indicates that respondents felt that the RCA was *more likely* to perform better than the alternatives for the various operational and personnel management objectives.

Analyzing how the alternatives perform with respect to each objective helps explain the outcome. Figure 3.3 shows the results of that analysis at the end of the second round. In this figure, we group results by objective, with each column representing the performance of a particular alternative with regard to that objective. As in Figure 3.2, the error bar at the top of each column represents the degree of convergence among panelists' assessments for that round.

These results indicate that panelists preferred the RCA because they considered it more likely to perform better with respect to regional security cooperation and regional contingency operations than the baseline. Consequently, it was considered better able to meet combatant commanders' operational needs. It fared only slightly worse with respect to other objectives than the baseline, including global contingency operations. The RDA performed about as well as the RCA with respect to operational objectives but worse with respect to global contingency operations and the personnel management objectives. In other words, the panelists believed that the RCA would perform better for the regional operations envisioned under RAF but incur only slightly greater risk for other objectives.

Results: Practitioner Interviews Emphasized Functional Expertise

The interviews we conducted with practitioners were consistent with this analysis and provide additional nuance. Although they acknowledged the potential utility of language, regional, and cultural expertise in the RAF context, practitioners generally accorded higher importance to functional expertise in soldiers' primary CMFs, at least for the execution of military engagement tasks. Additionally, respondents indicated that current pre-mission training adequately addressed any requirements for regional expertise. As indicated in Chapter Two, however, the experience on which these observations rest is almost entirely tactical in nature, mostly at the brigade level and below. Other respondents, however, stressed that it was important for soldiers and organizations with operational- and strategic-level responsibilities—e.g., theater-level logistics or communications—to understand how the unique requirements of their theaters of operations affected the employment of military capabilities. Additionally, respondents assigned to the USPACOM AOR stressed the importance of establishing and maintaining long-term relationships in identifying and leveraging opportunities for military engagement.

Interview respondents generally agreed with the panel that language, regional, and cultural skills were very useful in the RAF context, particularly for soldiers in such CMFs as military intelligence, signal, and logistics. Respondents believed that such skills and experience would also be useful for a variety of other fields, including

Figure 3.3
Panelists' Assessment of Alternative Personnel Management Concepts' Performance with Regard to Key Objectives: Expected Value of Each Alternative for Each Objective, Round 2

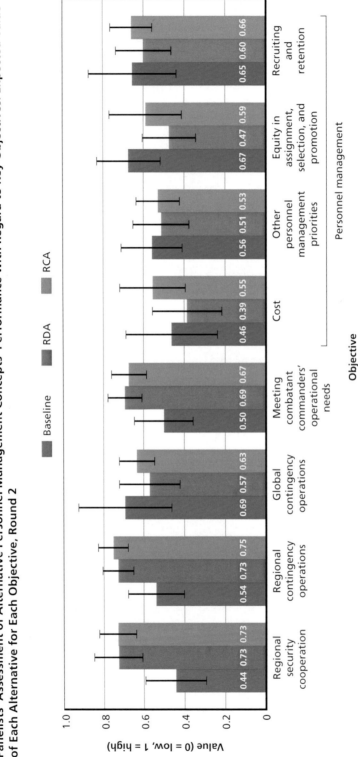

NOTE: The error bar at the top of each column indicates the degree of convergence among panel members' assessments in round 2.

RAND RR1065-3.3

field artillery, engineers, aviation, medical, legal, law enforcement, and public affairs specialists.[3] Respondents indicated that regional expertise would be especially useful for theater-level enabling functions, as embodied in various Army theater-level commands, e.g., theater sustainment commands, theater signal commands, theater intelligence brigades, and strategic signal brigades. These observations generally applied to planners and other staff positions at the division level and higher, in which incumbents would be concerned with shaping the theater for the employment of U.S. forces and identifying opportunities to further U.S. interests through military engagement.

Yet, although interviewees clearly valued regional expertise, they placed a far higher value on functional expertise. Most respondents asserted that RAF units were functioning effectively with very limited levels of regional expertise. Respondents from several Army service component commands noted that partners were more concerned about Army forces' functional expertise in military operations than about their ability to understand and navigate partners' cultures. One general officer with experience in AFRICOM remarked, "Our partners can build their own infantry but often lack the skills to provide the backbone of operational sustainment."

Respondents at several Army service component commands also indicated that, to the degree that any modicum of regional expertise might be required, the Army could provide that expertise in the course of pre-mission training. One respondent suggested that a two-week cultural immersion course should suffice and could be incorporated into the theater's reception, staging, onward movement, and integration process, such as that conducted at the Joint Multinational Training Command in Germany. Another respondent thought that soldiers could acquire the necessary skills through self-study.

We must interpret these observations with circumspection. As noted in Chapter Two, the Army has actually acquired very little experience with RAF *per se*, though the Army's recent experience with extensive counterinsurgency might apply to some degree. The experience practitioners have acquired is mostly at the tactical level and reflects only one model of preparing forces for those missions. Respondents have not had the opportunity to assess the relative effectiveness of units that employed different training models in similar missions.

One particularly important insight emerged during the panel deliberations. In previous discussions on this topic, participants had tended to assume that acquiring regional expertise would conflict with acquiring functional expertise, based on the example provided by the Afghanistan–Pakistan (AFPAK) Hands program. In that program, officers received substantial additional training and repetitive tours in selected billets in that theater of operations to enable them to become and function as experts

---

[3] Respondents also indicated that civilian-acquired skills presumed to be resident in the Army's RCs, such as law enforcement and legal services, would also be useful in the context of military engagement and enhanced by regional expertise.

in regional conditions. In many cases, an assignment as an AFPAK Hand came at the cost of an assignment of one or more key and developmental positions required for further promotion. Under RAF, however, soldiers would still pursue the same developmental path in terms of function but do so in a particular region.

Certainly, even following prescribed career models in a single regional context can prove limiting. Different kinds of forces—e.g., heavy armored forces—might be unevenly distributed in terms of regional alignment, limiting soldiers' experience in training with and employing these capabilities. The emphasis on different tactical and operational missions, such as the relative importance of decisive maneuver or military engagement, might differ by region as well. Although the career risks entailed in acquiring regional expertise might not equal those entailed by the AFPAK Hands program, it would not come without cost.

Implications

To the extent that practitioners and panel members' assessments are valid, they are not irreconcilable. Practitioners indicated that tactical units can perform acceptably in the RAF context with relatively low levels of regional expertise. They seemed to agree with our panelists, however, that additional levels of regional expertise might be useful in organizations with operational-level responsibilities, e.g., headquarters that might have to function as JTFs and theater-level enablers, such as theater intelligence brigades. Key billets include planners and those with a focus at operational and higher levels, such as theater logistics distribution, spectrum management, or combatant command staffs.

Assessing the Regional Cadre Alternative's Implications for Regional Expertise Requirements

To estimate the potential scope and scale of the requirement, the next step was to translate the general personnel concept into the number and type of billets that might require regional expertise. To do this, we used the following process:

1. **Identify the unit types of interest.** In general, these positions were either headquarters at or above the division echelon or theater-level enablers. We identified the following unit types: Army elements in combatant command headquarters, theater army headquarters, corps headquarters, division headquarters, theater sustainment commands, expeditionary sustainment commands, theater signal commands, theater strategic signal brigades, theater tactical signal brigades, theater intelligence brigades, and theater Army generating force organizations.
2. **Identify the positions within those units that fell into one of the categories we identified as of potential interest.** The overarching criterion for selecting a position was that regional conditions would significantly affect how military

capabilities provided or managed by the staff section or organization could be employed in that theater. For example, the degree to which private-sector logistical support is available differs extensively by region and within regions. The other criterion used was redundancy, in that we identified at least two soldiers in each staff section or organization, the senior officer, and the senior NCO. We assumed that each element required a critical mass of regional expertise in order to function effectively. The positions meeting these criteria were staff directors (e.g., with U.S. Joint Chiefs of Staff Manpower and Personnel Directorate or G-1s), deputy staff directors, planners, intelligence analysts, intelligence-collection managers, spectrum managers, operational logistics managers (e.g., distribution or transportation), public affairs officers, network operations managers, lawyers responsible for dealing with host-nation authorities, contracting officials, and world-religion chaplains.

3. **Determine the number of each unit type associated with each combatant command's AOR.**
4. **Multiply the number of billets in each unit type by the number of those units required in each theater.**

Results: The Regional Cadre Alternative Has Implications for Regional Expertise Requirements

We intend the lists of unit and position types to be illustrative, not exhaustive. We provide them to illustrate the basis for our estimates, not to recommend that these particular positions be designated as requiring regional expertise.

If one accepts the reasoning by which this list was developed, however, it leads to the quantities indicated in Figure 3.1 at the beginning of this chapter, a total of approximately 4,300 commissioned officers, WOs, and enlisted soldiers.

Conclusion

Two important findings emerge from this analysis. The first is that **acquiring appropriate regional expertise need not conflict with normal career progression, at least not substantially.** Most stakeholders simply assumed that acquiring regional expertise could come only at the cost of functional experience. The AFPAK Hands program is often cited as an example. Whether that model is to be embraced or avoided depends on one's perspective and is not addressed here. The perception is widely shared that service as an AFPAK Hand was detrimental to a soldier's career progression. Whether that perception is accurate, the analogy is inapt. The AFPAK Hands program assigned soldiers—and sailors, airmen, and marines—to nontraditional jobs outside of traditional career development tracks. To the extent that RAF might affect career management, however, it will do so by requiring soldiers to perform jobs already on their career tracks, albeit in a particular region. The fact that it is possible to align the acquisition of regional expertise with the acquisition of functional expertise does not mean that doing so entails no marginal costs, either to individual soldiers' careers or to the Army's inventory of functional expertise.

The second significant finding is that **the scope and scale of the requirement for such expertise are likely to be manageable.** To the extent that regional expertise might be required, it will be needed for select positions in headquarters and theater-level enablers. We estimate the total requirement at about 4,300 commissioned officers, NCOs, and WOs. By way of comparison, we note that the Army projects more than 200,000 soldiers in the relevant grades (mostly NCOs) in fiscal year 2015. The ratio of billets requiring regional expertise to the overall number of soldiers in the right grades makes the problem appear to be quite manageable on its face. In the next chapter, we analyze this issue in greater depth.

As discussed in Chapter Two, these findings unavoidably rest on tenuous empirical bases. Army forces have accrued relatively little experience in a narrow slice of the full range of military operations envisioned under the RAF context. That experience has been accrued mostly at the maneuver brigade level and below. It is altogether possible that extended experience with military engagement missions in the RAF context will demonstrate that regional expertise at tactical levels is critical to the success of future operations. It is also possible that such experience will indicate that significantly increasing soldiers' regional expertise provides only marginal benefits in terms of mission success. We cannot predict with any great confidence which of these outcomes is likely to obtain over the long term.

In spite of these limitations, this analysis still represents an explicit, rigorous balancing of costs and benefits. The expert panel we convened assessed the RCA as likely to accrue most of the benefits of increasing regional expertise at the lowest costs to other objectives—notably, the Army's ability to support global contingency operations. That finding is consistent with the testimony of various Army officials with whom we spoke. Whether the empirical grounds on which the panel made this assessment are especially solid, they still provide better support to this course of action than they do to more-ambitious measures, such as the RDA considered in this analysis.

As Army forces accrue more experience in a fuller range of military operations under RAF, it will be important to revisit this question. Analysts should pursue several lines of inquiry. Possible research approaches include comparing case studies in U.S. and allied employment of conventional forces for security cooperation activities, a review of regionally aligned units' after-action reports, or surveys of personnel from those units. With regard to surveys, a stated-preference approach—in which respondents are asked to make trade-offs between various goods—would be useful in assessing the value of regional experience relative to other goods.

CHAPTER FOUR

Assessing the Army's Ability to Develop Regional Expertise

In this chapter, we present a way for the Army to assess personnel management policies' capacity to support the regional qualification system described in Chapter Three. To do so, we developed a prototype of a metric-based approach for estimating and tracking the number of soldiers with varying degrees of regional alignment experience. The information derived from these processes could be used to assist the personnel community in determining whether it has sufficient inventory—with the right distribution of regional experiences—to support current and future personnel assignment demands.

As we describe in this chapter, our simulation of soldiers' accumulation of regional experience using historical assignment patterns suggests that the Army will likely accrue sufficient inventories of soldiers with relevant regional expertise to meet the modest demands estimated in Chapter Three, at least as long as the Army's end strength and posture approximate current conditions. The challenge will be to match the soldiers who have accumulated the required experience with the billets requiring it. We also provide examples of what the Army might learn and track about the breadth and depth of regional experience—from the individual soldier to the entire force—if the Army decided to track regional identifiers in its data systems. We define breadth as the number of regions in which soldiers have acquired a meaningful degree of experience; we define depth as the degree of experience soldiers have acquired in a particular region. For the purposes of this analysis, we measure both breadth and depth in terms of the number of assignments to a given region and the aggregate duration of those assignments.

We do not wish to imply that soldiers acquire either breadth or depth solely through their military assignments and education. For example, immigrants' depth in a particular region and culture can start at birth and be largely complete before they even join the Army. We focus on the number of assignments because *that is what we can measure in our simulation*. If the Army can produce a sufficient number of soldiers with the required degree of regional expertise relying solely on assignments, then it almost certainly can achieve the number required in the real world, where it can leverage talent accrued in many other contexts. If our simulation were to indicate that the Army could not produce sufficient numbers of soldiers with the required experience on the basis of their assignment histories, that result would not indicate that producing enough experts would be impossible but rather that the Army might have to recruit more heavily from immigrant communities.

Research Approach

We approached this issue by simulating how the Army's normal assignment processes would distribute regional experience under steady-state conditions. We needed to simulate this process because relatively few soldiers have acquired significant regional experience outside of the CENTCOM AOR for well over a decade. Instead, we analyzed soldiers' assignment records to evaluate the regional experience they would have acquired *if* the units in which they served had been regionally aligned.

For each soldier, we computed metrics for both breadth and depth. *Breadth* refers to the number of unique regionally aligned assignments the soldier would have, while *depth* refers to the number of years the soldier was aligned with a region. We computed the latter metric for each region. With these metrics in hand, we compare the number of soldiers who would have acquired a certain degree of regional experience and the billets requiring such experience in each theater. In sum, this analysis enables analysis of

- the number of unique regionally aligned assignments soldiers would have (*breadth*)
- the number of years soldiers were aligned with regions (*depth*)
- the distribution of soldiers with specified degrees of regional experience by combatant commands' AORs (*depth by location*)
- variation in depth across CMFs (*depth by career assignment area*).

Because we were looking at soldiers' past experiences and the Army personnel system has not maintained records pertaining to soldiers' regional alignments, the approach we present in this chapter is a prototype, and our findings do not represent or portray the true number of personnel with specific amounts of regional experience. To do so would require the Army to tag soldiers' personnel records with information indicating affiliation with a unit aligned with a region or, better yet, direct experience operating in a region.

Determining Regional Alignment

For purposes of this demonstration, we determined that soldiers were aligned with specific regions based on their historical assignment patterns derived from soldiers' units or installations. That is, we matched units or installations to hypothetical regional alignments (e.g., 1st Infantry Division and AFRICOM). Table 4.1 shows the unit- or installation-to-region mapping that we used for the analyses. We then aligned soldiers with regions based on the units or installations to which they were assigned.

Table 4.1
Projecting Current Assignment Patterns onto Hypothetical Regional Alignments

Division or Corps and Installation	Regional Alignment
1st ID, Fort Riley, Kansas	AFRICOM
10th ID, Fort Drum, New York	AFRICOM
1st Armored Division, Fort Bliss, Texas	CENTCOM
1st Cavalry Division, Fort Hood, Texas	CENTCOM
4th ID, Fort Carson, Colorado	CENTCOM
III Corps, Fort Hood, Texas	CENTCOM
2nd ID, Korea and Joint Base Lewis-McChord, Washington	USPACOM
25th ID, Hawaii	USPACOM
I Corps, Joint Base Lewis-McChord, Washington	USPACOM
82nd Airborne Division, Fort Bragg, North Carolina	GRF
101st Airborne Division, Fort Campbell, Kentucky	GRF
3rd ID, Fort Steward, Georgia	GRF
XVIII Airborne Corps, Fort Bragg, North Carolina	GRF

Note that the notional alignment assumes that all assets typically associated with those headquarters share their alignment, something not necessarily the case in real life. Not shown are the table of distribution and allowance organizations, such as Joint Multinational Training Command at Grafenwoehr, Germany, which are also regionally aligned, though our analysis also accounted for such organizations. By tracking soldiers' assignments to units associated with these headquarters and other regionally aligned unit identification codes (UICs), we could measure the number of regions with which they would have been aligned and the duration of such alignments over the course of their careers.

Calculating Breadth and Depth

We calculated breadth and depth measures for each enlisted soldier and officer in the database. Breadth is a function of the number of regional alignments. Out of a maximum of six regional alignments, greatest breadth is achieved when a soldier has been assigned to units aligned to each of the six regions. We constructed depth-ratio scores for each region to indicate the number of years a soldier was aligned with a region as a share of total years in service.[1] Thus, depth scores can be constructed for all soldiers and then compared across CMFs and pay grades in any or all regions. To obtain a crude measure of the degree of selectivity possible under current policies, we compared the distribution of soldiers by the resulting depth ratios and the current requirements for soldiers with the appropriate grades and CMFs.

The notional regional alignment used for this analysis was close but not identical to the regional alignment described in unclassified Army presentations in late 2013.[2] There are notable differences, however. Rather than assess a specific regional alignment pattern, which was not appropriate given the evolving nature of unit alignment with regions, we instead looked to assess current Army personnel management policies' general capacity to support regional alignment. We acknowledge that Army policy is to rotate regional alignments, at least at the brigade level and below, but did not attempt to model this dynamic. This rotation would undoubtedly complicate the process of assessing requirements for regional alignment and soldiers' accumulation of regional experience. Our assessments should thus be considered an upper bound.

Data analysis began by tracing soldiers' assignment histories each year using UICs, then retroactively aligning UICs with a region (see Table 4.1), and finally, for each year in the database, assigning a soldier to a region based on this matching process. We repeated this process for each officer and soldier by CMF. For each person, we developed a regional alignment history that included the number of alignments through the career, years in each region, and when alignment occurred during the course of the career.

The analysis presented in this chapter focuses on this select group of CMFs (the CMF code is in parentheses):

- infantry (11)
- engineer (12)
- field artillery (13)
- aviation (15)
- armor (19)
- signal (25)
- military intelligence (35)
- psychological operations (37)
- medical (68)
- supply (92).

---

[1]   Using years of service accounts for time spent in other regions, as well as time spent not regionally aligned, and thus is a more-accurate picture of how much depth a soldier or officer has in a particular region relative to his or her total time in service.

[2]   Units' regional alignments have continued to evolve and change during this study. As a result, the unit- or installation-to-region alignments used could be different from those at the time of this writing.

This list is broadly representative of the variety of CMFs seen within the Army, which includes both combat and support career fields. It includes career fields that require a range of skills, as well as those with specialized skills and expertise.

Data

We extracted relevant data from the Total Army Personnel Database (TAPDB), including unit assignment information with historical records covering the period 1989 to 2013.

Results: Description of the Population

We begin with basic information about our population of interest (Figure 4.1), which included the ten CMFs listed above. This population included more than 30,000 officers and almost 247,000 enlisted personnel. Despite this distribution, we restricted the majority of our analysis to the 118,311 E-5s, E-6s, and E-7s and the 19,905 O-3s, O-4s, and O-5s in 2013 because these personnel are likely to support regional missions in key leader or staff assignments, and they have had enough years of service to have developed wide breadth or substantial depth (or both). Among O-3s to O-5s, close to 60 percent are O-3s, and close to half of enlisted personnel in the E-5 to E-7 pay grades are E-5s. Figure 4.1 illustrates the distribution of pay grade for our chosen group of

Figure 4.1
Population Distribution, by Rank, E-5–E-7 and O-3–O-5

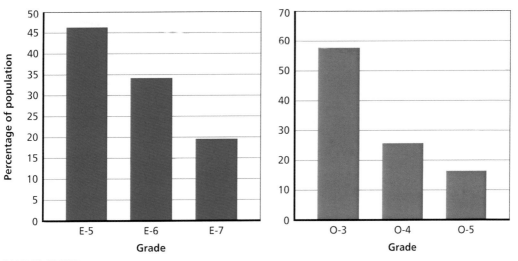

SOURCE: TAPDB.
NOTE: Data are for the 118,311 E-5s, E-6s, and E-7s and 19,905 O-3s, O-4s, and O-5s.
RAND RR1065-4.1

CMFs. Not surprisingly, the population was dominated by more junior officers and enlisted personnel.

Figure 4.2 details the allocation of the population by CMF. We can see that the largest group, at around 27,021, is made up of infantry (CMF 11), followed by supply (92) at 19,264, medical personnel (68) at 13,959, and audiovisual (25) at 16,611 enlisted and officer personnel.

Unless otherwise noted, the analyses presented in this chapter include all ten CMFs (E-5–E-7 and O-3–O-5) as described above.

Results: Breadth of Regional Alignment Experience

First, we examined breadth of regional experience among the enlisted and commissioned-officer populations. For this analysis, we defined breadth as the number of regions to which soldiers were matched during their careers. A soldier would have little regional breadth if he was matched to a single region in his career; conversely, matching to six regions in a career would be a large amount of breadth. Breadth is independent of the length of assignments or the number of times assigned to regions. As an example, under this definition, an assignment to one USPACOM-aligned unit and one U.S. European Command–aligned unit count as two degrees of breadth, while two assignments to USPACOM-aligned units would count as one degree of

Figure 4.2
Relative Allocation of the Personnel Data Set, by Career Management Field,
E-5–E-7 and O-3–O-5

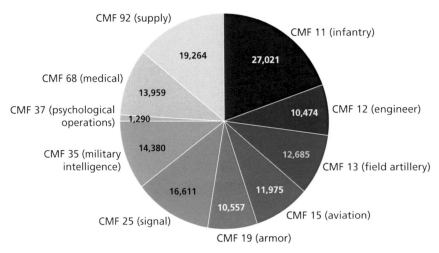

SOURCE: TAPDB.
NOTE: The data are for 138,216 commissioned officers and NCOs.
RAND RR1065-4.2

breadth. Regional breadth therefore is one metric that can be used to evaluate the breadth of experience that is resident in the Army.

Figure 4.3 displays the percentages of NCOs (E-5 to E-7) and commissioned officers (O-3 to O-5) who had up to five regional assignments during their careers. We found that, for both enlisted and officer personnel, the bulk of the distribution showed a peak at one regional alignment. In addition, approximately 70 percent of the commissioned officers and 65 percent of the NCOs had either one or two regional alignments. These findings suggest that, if unit and installation were similar to that in Table 4.1 and if no other personnel actions were taken, the vast majority of mid–senior-level personnel would have a low level of regional breadth and most likely a higher level of regional depth. We would expect that earlier-career personnel would have fewer regional alignments, on average, than later-career personnel because they have been in the service for a shorter period and have not had the opportunity to accumulate alignments.

To see whether early-career personnel had fewer regional alignments, we conducted similar analyses for each of the pay-grade groups in our population. The results of these analyses are in Figures 4.4 and 4.5. Our expectation that senior personnel—that is, those with more years of service—were more likely to have greater breadth than lower-rank personnel was correct. For example, the values in Figure 4.4 show that 41 percent of the E-5s had worked in only one region, whereas the percentage of E-7s having worked in only one region was half of that seen for E-5s—19 percent. On the other hand, although 43 percent of E-5s had two or more regional alignments, 75 per-

Figure 4.3
Percentage of Personnel Having Various Levels of Alignment Breadth, E-5–E-7 and O-3–O-5

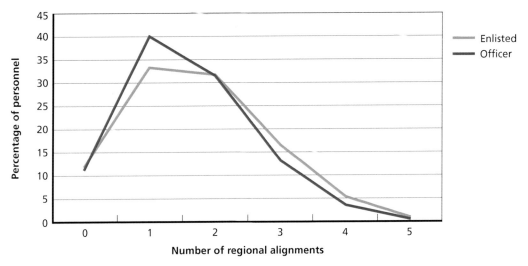

SOURCE: TAPDB.
NOTE: Data are for the 118,311 E-5s, E-6s, and E-7s and 19,905 O-3s, O-4s, and O-5s.
RAND RR1065-4.3

Figure 4.4
Percentage of Enlisted Personnel Having Various Levels of Alignment Breadth, by Pay Grade, E-5–E-7

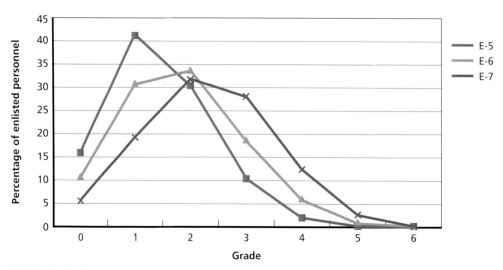

SOURCE: TAPDB.
NOTE: Data are for the 118,311 E-5s, E-6s, and E-7s.
RAND RR1065-4.4

Figure 4.5
Percentage of Officer Personnel Having Various Levels of Alignment Breadth, by Pay Grade, O-3–O-5

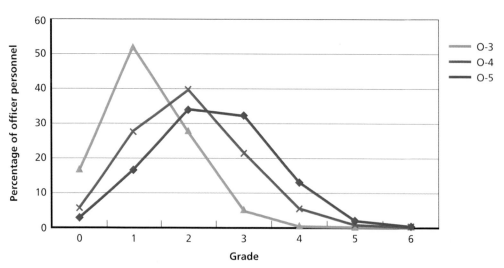

SOURCE: TAPDB.
NOTE: Data are for the 19,905 O-3s, O-4s, and O-5s.
RAND RR1065-4.5

cent of E-7s had two or more regional alignments. It is important to note that the bulk of these multiple regional alignments among E-7s are accounted for by just two or three regional alignments (60 percent of E-7s).

We found similar breadth results for officers (Figure 4.5). Proportionally fewer senior officers (O-5) had one or two regional alignments (50 percent) than O-3 (79 percent) or O-4 (67 percent). More than 80 percent of O-5s had multiple regional alignments (two or more), whereas only 32 percent of O-3s had the same. Similar to what we found for NCOs, the bulk of multiple regional alignments among O-5s were accounted for by just two or three regional alignments (66 percent). Even though regional breadth increased as more years of service were completed, large percentages of officers remained who appeared to retain some regional depth by being assigned to just one or two regions. We explore depth later in this chapter.

We also examined breadth differences across CMFs and between the NCO (Table 4.2) and commissioned-officer (Table 4.3) samples. We found some modest differences among CMFs for NCOs. For example, more than 60 percent of armor personnel (CMF 19) and close to 70 percent of medical personnel (CMF 68) had two or

Table 4.2
Percentage of Enlisted Personnel Having Various Levels of Alignment Breadth, E-5–E-7

Number of Regional Alignments	CMF									
	11	12	13	15	19	25	35	37	68	92
None	16	10	10	14	5	12	25	0.2	6	8
One	38	37	33	35	32	32	41	61	25	27
Two or more	46	53	57	52	64	55	35	39	68	65

SOURCE: TAPDB.

NOTE: Some columns do not add up to 100 because of rounding. Data are for the 118,311 E-5s, E-6s, and E-7s.

Table 4.3
Percentage of Officer Personnel Having Various Levels of Alignment Breadth, O-3–O-5

Number of Regional Alignments	CMF									
	11	12	13	15	19	25	35	37	68	92
None	14	10	9	15	6	10	10	1	22	24
One	44	40	35	40	39	37	40	28	59	53
Two or more	42	50	56	45	55	53	50	71	19	23

SOURCE: TAPDB.

NOTE: Data are for the 19,905 O-3s, O-4s, and O-5s.

more regional alignments. On the other hand, fewer than half of infantry (CMF 11), military intelligence (CMF 35), and psychological operations (CMF 37) had two or more regional alignments.

For commissioned officers, the pattern was generally the same as that for NCOs, with a few exceptions. More than 70 percent of psychological operations (CMF 37) personnel had two or more regional alignments. Some of the most striking differences occurred between medical (CMF 68) and supply (CMF 92) officers and all other sub-groups: Fewer than 20 percent of medical personnel and 23 percent of supply officers had two or more alignments, as compared with all other groups (42 to 71 percent).

The analysis above sheds some light on the potential regional breadth of Army personnel. The majority of commissioned officers and NCOs had between one and two regional alignments. This suggests that there might be greater depth than breadth force-wide. A soldier's pay grade was a key determinant of breadth of experience, with higher pay grades possessing greater breadth, but there are also some differences by CMF. We next discuss our analysis of depth under the RAF context.

Results: Depth of Regional Alignment Experience

We now turn our attention to measuring soldiers' depth of regional experience across pay grade, CMF, and regions, with the goal of answering three key questions:

- How much depth could Army personnel accumulate, and does it vary by pay grade and CMF?
- Would unit or installation regional alignment practices produce a sufficient inventory of personnel with adequate levels of regional expertise?
- In what ways does timing of experience matter, and how might it be factored in?

We sought to determine the extent of soldiers' levels of regional expertise given a regional alignment framework that assigns soldiers to units or installations aligned to regions. Although we do not discuss how the Army could address perceived lack of depth, the method we employed in the analysis could be used to identify lack of adequate regional depth in one or more regions and thus would indicate where to focus remediation or change. Moreover, this analysis brings to the forefront questions about how important timing is to accruing relevant regional experience. Finally, we assess the extent to which depth varies by CMF using the prescribed alignment strategy from Table 4.1 to highlight where there might be greater gaps in one CMF versus another and whether the education, training, and assignment systems might be changed to ensure that CMFs with low levels of depth could be improved.

In answering the questions above, we employ two related but distinct metrics:

- *time spent per alignment*, which is derived from the total number of years aligned with a region. This measure is a simple average of the amount of time spent in each region.
- *depth-ratio score (time spent aligned as a share of total years of service in a region)*, which is the relative share of time spent in a particular region. In this case, a depth-ratio score would be computed for each region and indicates the amount of time a soldier spent in a particular region as a share of the length of that person's career in the Army.

Together, these two metrics tell us whether some regions are better represented than others, given the approach we took to determine regional alignment, and how regions compare relative to one another in share of total years of service. Consistently with the approach discussed previously in this chapter, we use assignment to a unit or installation as a proxy for a soldier's regional alignment. Recall that, for each year of record, we identified the unit or installation to which soldiers were assigned and matched the soldier to a region based on this assignment.

Distribution of Regional Depth

We analyzed NCO data from two regions; the results are presented in Figure 4.6.[3] The average number of years in regional alignment spent in CENTCOM was greater than for AFRICOM across all CMFs. Even within regions, the average number of years spent in regional alignment varied by CMF. Regional alignment in both CENTCOM and AFRICOM was lowest for psychological operations (CMF 37) and highest in CENTCOM for field artillery (CMF 13) and medical (CMF 68), at close to 4.5 years regionally aligned, and in AFRICOM for infantry (CMF 11) and aviation (CMF 15) at 3.5 years regionally aligned.

Figure 4.6 illustrates the point that the amount of time spent in a region varied by CMF. Moreover, between the two chosen regions, all CMFs spent more time, on average, aligned with CENTCOM than with AFRICOM. Focusing on one pay grade, we can see in Figure 4.7 that E-7s were aligned for greater periods of time with CENTCOM and USAREUR, at close to 4.5 years, compared with just less than two years in Korea.

The patterns described above largely held for commissioned officers as well.

The previous analyses provided very broad perspectives about depth across and within regions, CMFs, or pay grades. They do not, however, provide detailed information as to the distribution of depth by region, pay grade, and CMF. We developed the

---

[3]   Because this is a simulation, we do not provide simulation findings for all possible combinations. Instead, we provide illustrative findings that demonstrate the approach and how the approach and its results could be used to support policy and program decisions.

Figure 4.6
Average Number of Years Spent in U.S. Africa Command and U.S. Central Command, by Career Management Field, E-5–E-7

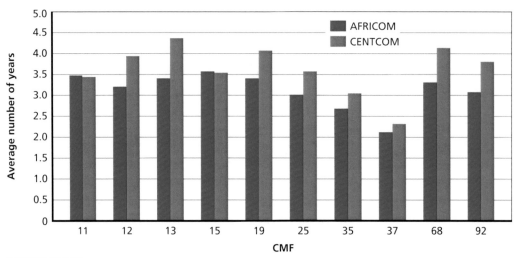

SOURCE: TAPDB.
NOTE: Data are for the 18,914 soldiers aligned with AFRICOM and the 49,213 soldiers aligned with CENTCOM. They do not include soldiers with no regional alignments.
RAND RR1065-4.6

Figure 4.7
Average Number of Years Aligned for E-7s, by Region, All Career Management Fields

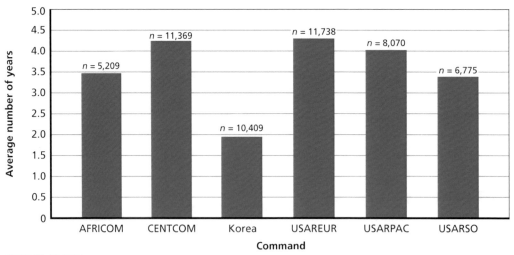

SOURCE: TAPDB.
RAND RR1065-4.7

depth-ratio metric to calculate the share of time a soldier spent in each region relative to that soldier's time in the service. This metric allows us to determine how many soldiers by grade, CMF, or any other factor of interest have specific levels of regional depth.

Figure 4.8 is an illustrative example of this depth-ratio metric. For this analysis, we looked at the population of O-3s to O-5s by region. For this sample, we computed their depth-ratio metric scores. We group the values on the horizontal axis by region, and we organized the proportion of officers' depth scores by region into approximately 10th-percentile groupings (0.01 to 0.09, 0.10 to 0.19, 0.20 to 0.29, 0.30 to 0.39, and greater than 0.39).

The distribution of depth ratios varied considerably across regions. In all regions, except AFRICOM and Korea, the largest number of officers had depth ratios between 0.10 and 0.19. In other words, in terms of depth by region, the majority of those officers who were assigned to units aligned with regions had spent approximately 10 to 19 percent of their careers in specific regions—a relatively low level of depth relative to what is possible. However, many officers had greater levels of depth. Take the case of CENTCOM, where 7 percent of the officers had relatively low levels of CENTCOM experience—only spending 1 to 9 percent of their careers in units aligned with that

Figure 4.8
Depth Ratios for Commissioned Officers, by Region, O-3s–O-5s

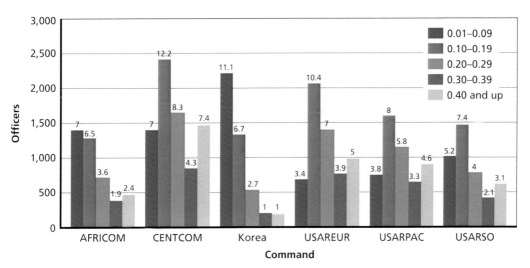

SOURCE: TAPDB.
NOTE: We excluded from the chart soldiers with no regional depth. Value labels are the total percentages by depth score category and include soldiers with no alignments. The sum of the percentages represents the total percentage of soldiers having spent at least one year in alignment. The remainder represents soldiers who were not aligned with that particular region. Approximately 15,600, 12,100, 15,400, 14,000, 14,840, and 15,600 soldiers were not aligned with that particular region, respectively.
RAND RR1065-4.8

region. On the other hand, 12 percent of all officers had spent 30 percent or more of their careers in units aligned with CENTCOM. Excluding officers with no alignments, the percentages were 18 percent with low levels of CENTCOM experience versus 30 percent with higher levels of CENTCOM experience.

In fact, we saw similar trends and distributions for most regions (AFRICOM and Korea are the exceptions). So the depth metric can be used to understand the level of depth down to the soldier level or aggregated up to CMF, grade, or the entire force. The metric also can be used to understand whether the current or future personnel inventory can adequately meet future requirements. In the next subsection, we explore what this process would look like.

Assessment of Potential Inventory Against Estimated Requirements

To examine whether current Army policies support sufficient inventory, we used our computed depth ratios, which explain the amount of time spent in a region as a share of total years of service. This metric can be used to compare the distribution of soldiers by depth with the personnel requirements by CMF and pay grade. To do this, we used the requirement estimate described in Chapter Two and detailed in the appendix, and then generated a distribution of soldiers by depth score. Taking the number of soldiers required, we determined the minimum depth score at which the number of required soldiers was met. The results are illustrated in Figure 4.9.

Figure 4.9
Distribution of U.S. Central Command Depth Ratios for O-5, Career Management Field 25, Signal

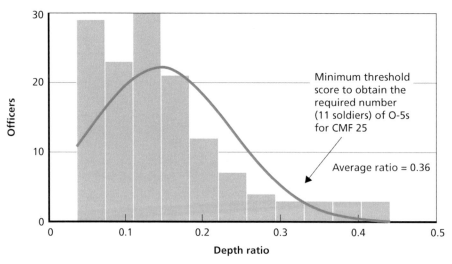

SOURCE: TAPDB and analysis of Army authorization documents.
RAND RR1065-4.9

In this case, we looked at a subset of CMFs that included O-5s. We obtained demand counts by region, as described in Chapter Three, and then determined whether sufficient inventory existed. Our analysis assumed that the Army would fill vacant positions with soldiers possessing the highest degree of regional experience from the pool of O-5s from the relevant CMFs. We then computed the minimum depth score among the officers used to fill those vacancies and the average depth score for that group. For CMF 25 O-5s, for example, 11 soldiers were required who would have CENTCOM experience. Comparing that with our distribution, we found that, if 11 were selected, the minimum score would be 0.30, with a mean of 0.36. Assuming that the length of the average O-5's career was 19 years, that would mean that the least experienced O-5 selected would have accumulated 5.7 years in the region, while the average O-5 would have accumulated 6.8 years.

In Table 4.4, we present an example table of requirements and depth-ratio scores for O-5s across all regions and CMFs. Drawing on our current method of aligning soldiers with regions based on the units to which they were assigned, the minimum threshold score for that number of soldiers was 0.35—that is, at least 11 soldiers were at or above that depth score. The average depth score for that group of soldiers was 0.3. This exercise can be repeated for every pay grade and CMF, for both commissioned officers and NCOs, to determine the range and average regional experience that a group of soldiers will have, given the requirements and the method used to align soldiers with regions.

The Importance of Timing

The measures of *time spent in a region* and *time spent in a region relative to total time in a soldier's career* tell us something about depth, but it might also be the *timing* of that experience that matters. If the majority of alignments occur during the early career period, then those experiences might be out of date and no longer relevant at the more-senior stages of a career. Moreover, accumulation of alignments during early phases of a career could mean fewer total aligned senior-level personnel at a future period. Although we did not analyze this issue here, an additional metric could be developed, which is the *number of years aligned to a specific region most recently in a career*, e.g., in the past five years as a measure of currency of alignment. The data reveal that, for both enlisted and officer personnel, the middle grades were a key turning point in terms of acquiring regional expertise. Over time, these alignments become distributed across multiple regions, thereby reducing depth in any one region. Thus, a depth measure that captures the timing of alignment could be a useful way to distinguish between experience that was acquired recently and that acquired some time back. Needless to say, results for such a measure might vary by CMF.

Table 4.4
Supply Requirements and Depth Ratios, by Career Management Field and Command, for O-5s

CMF	AFRICOM			CENTCOM			USAREUR			USARPAC			USARSO		
	Required	Depth Ratio		Required	Depth Ratio		Required	Depth Ratio		Required	Depth Ratio		Required	Depth Ratio	
		Min.	Avg.		Min.	Avg.		Min.	Avg.		Min.	Avg.		Min.	Avg.
11	0	n/a	n/a	0	n/a	n/a	1	0.63	0.63	2	0.48	0.57	0	n/a	n/a
12	2	0.32	0.35	4	0.38	0.46	5	0.38	0.45	4	0.42	0.45	1	0.29	0.29
13	2	0.43	0.44	3	0.56	0.58	3	0.57	0.71	4	1.00	1.00	1	1.00	1.00
15	1	0.4	0.4	1	0.55	0.55	3	0.47	0.52	1	0.48	0.48	1	0.44	0.44
25	2	0.23	0.25	11	0.3	0.36	17	0.35	0.45	10	0.25	0.34	1	0.29	0.29
35	12	0.24	0.30	24	0.22	0.28	20	0.33	0.42	25	0.22	0.32	8	0.22	0.27
37	2	0.21	0.23	3	0.27	0.32	3	0.21	0.22	2	0.38	0.39	1	0.23	0.23

SOURCE: TAPDB and the Army Authorization Document System.

NOTE: n/a = not applicable (when the required number is 0, the minimum and the average achievable are irrelevant).

Implications for Depth and Breadth

These analyses are simulated in that soldiers' regional alignment was based on a notional alignment of units and installations to regions. Nevertheless, this analysis illustrates the types of findings and insights that could be learned and tracked with respect to the balance of breadth and depth from the soldier up to force-wide, if the Army were tracking regional identifiers in its data systems.

Looking across all chosen CMFs but differentiating by pay grade, we found that the average time spent in any one regional alignment declined with the number of regional alignments. On average, enlisted personnel spent more time in alignment than officers. We also found that, at any given number of regional alignments, the higher pay grades, on average across all CMFs, spent more time in regional alignments than the lower pay grades. These results in large part indicate that, as years of service increase, the opportunities to gain breadth and depth will naturally increase. For example, E-4s with four regional alignments spend an average of around two years in each regional alignment. On the other hand, E-7s with four regional alignments spend an average of 3.5 years per regional alignment.

Once years of service are accounted for, depth by region varied widely across soldiers—that is, some have extensive depth, whereas others have more breadth than depth. This simulation provided insights into how the Army can more precisely understand when and how breadth and depth occur in soldiers' careers and can also pinpoint by CMF, pay grade, or region which groups of soldiers need more or less regional experience and when in their careers. The approaches presented in this chapter could be used to support the assignment of soldiers based on regional experiences or to actively prevent personnel inventory shortages with respect to having enough people with the right experiences.

This simulation, furthermore, illustrates how the amount of soldier depth can be identified and then used to inform the personnel community that some CMFs or pay-grade groups have lower experience levels than others and then to compare these values with expected demand. Our supply and demand analysis did not identify any supply shortages, but again, these analyses are predicated on an alignment like the one in Table 4.1 and current expected demands. If either the supply (that is, regional matching) or the demand changes, the approaches in this chapter could be leveraged to understand whether the personnel system can provide an adequate number of soldiers and officers to meet the Army's needs. Similarly, they will also prove valuable in helping the Army develop appropriate goals, objectives, and criteria for the personnel management system to use in guiding development of required expertise.

Conclusion

Informed by the simplified analysis presented in this chapter, **we conclude that the Army can probably produce enough soldiers with relevant expertise to meet the modest demands estimated in Chapter Three**, at least as long as the Army maintains approximately the same end strength and posture. It is important to understand that the Army does not have an extensive inventory of soldiers with expertise in regions other than the CENTCOM AOR. Very few soldiers have had the opportunity to acquire significant experience in other regions at this point. It is thus necessary to estimate the inventory of soldiers with different regional experience that might accumulate over time.

Our simulation of soldiers' accumulation of regional experience using historical assignment patterns suggests that the Army will likely accrue sufficient inventories of such personnel after several years of RAF implementation. Depending on the degree of experience required, the Army should be able to fill positions with regionally experienced personnel and still retain a modicum of selectivity. **The problem that the Army will have to address is matching the soldiers who have accumulated the required experience with the billets requiring it.** Managing the development of regional knowledge and experience in selected soldiers will aid in and go hand-in-hand with this process, as we discuss in the next chapter.

CHAPTER FIVE

Tracking and Measuring Regionally Aligned Forces–Relevant Knowledge, Skills, and Abilities

The initial requirement for RAF expertise is likely to be modest, though the limited data on which that conclusion is based preclude certainty about that prediction. Our modeling indicates that the Army can probably produce enough soldiers with the requisite experience—a proxy for expertise—to meet that requirement. The problem is matching soldiers who have expertise with the positions that require it. As researchers at the Army War College's Strategic Studies Institute have found, that places managing soldiers to support RAF squarely within the larger context of talent management (Bukowski et al., 2014). This chapter proposes measures that can enable personnel managers to identify, track, and measure regional expertise and implement a talent management approach to support RAF.

DoD uses *LREC* to describe the range of organizational capabilities and individual competencies that enable effective operation in a dynamic global environment. Soldiers' LREC KSAOs potentially support the Army's implementation of the RAF concept, and the Army should therefore consider how to measure and track them. This idea is nothing new. *Department of Defense Strategic Plan for Language Skills, Regional Expertise, and Cultural Capabilities, 2011–2016* (Under Secretary of Defense for Personnel and Readiness, undated) identified the multiple systems that track language proficiency as the starting point for developing more-comprehensive measures of LREC training and skills. In 2011, the Defense Language and National Security Education Office tasked the RAND National Defense Research Institute and the MITRE Corporation to jointly address questions concerning DoD's ability to measure and track LREC KSAs. More narrowly, the U.S. Government Accountability Office completed a study in July 2014 that examined how the Army and Marine Corps identify and track personnel with security force assistance–related training, education, and experience.

In fact, the desire to track KSAs extends far beyond LREC. Soldiers, sailors, airmen, and marines have all sorts of civilian skills, degrees, and certifications, as well as unique operational experiences that are not inherent to their military occupations yet might improve mission effectiveness for the right unit at the right time. For example, the Army Green Pages[1] concept, piloted primarily by the U.S. Army Corps of Engineers from 2010 to 2012, sought to capture these KSAs and make them accessible to assignment officers and to units. In the mid-2000s, the Navy had an initiative called Sea Warrior that included an effort to track, among other things, each sailor's certifications, qualifications, professional and personal development milestones, and educational achievement.

Without imposing any new requirements today on the personnel system, the Army can take some low-cost, low-regret steps that will enable it to learn what personnel data are truly useful to regionally aligned units and to those developing and assigning soldiers with LREC and related KSAs. In this chapter, we explain how the Army can use personnel development skill identifiers (PDSIs) as a means of providing assignment managers and units basic, structured, standardized information about soldiers' RAF-relevant experience. Because of the limitations in how PDSIs are managed today, it might be necessary at the outset to limit awarding PDSIs only to soldiers in certain grades or CMFs. At some point in the future, this could lead to new, more-formal approaches to developing and managing LREC KSAs. But, for now, the Army would be prudent to have less ambitious goals of making RAF-relevant personnel information more standardized and accessible. Over time, the Army should put into place processes to assess how the PDSIs and other, less-structured data identify information about soldiers that ultimately correlates with personal performance and unit effectiveness.

Challenges to Tracking Regionally Relevant Knowledge, Skills, and Abilities

These efforts face two formidable challenges. The first is that KSAs other than those that are tied directly to military training, education, and experience are typically self-reported and difficult to validate. This is not to suggest that people deliberately misrepresent or exaggerate their skills, but, without established standards, tests, dates, and so forth, it can be very difficult to know what skills people really bring to a job and how current their knowledge is. The problem is amplified when KSAs relate to concepts as nebulous as regional expertise and culture.

A second challenge is that it can be difficult to know what KSAs really affect individual performance or unit effectiveness. The utility of a soldier's particular skills might depend greatly on the unit mission and that soldier's assigned tasks. It might

---

[1] The Army Green Pages concept established an internal labor market for officers in select CMFs. In the pilot program, units described their requirements in greater detail than commonly available to individual officers and personnel managers. Individual officers described their capabilities in greater detail than commonly available on their record briefs and identified preferences, while units described their needs and the opportunities available. Assignment managers leveraged this information to try to achieve the best fit between officers' specific capabilities and preferences and unit needs (Office of Economic and Manpower Analysis [OEMA], 2012).

not matter whether a specific person has a specific skill, just that somebody in the unit does. Alternatively, it could be that a unit makes a perfectly reasonable request for a soldier with a particular set of skills, given the position to be filled and the unit's mission, but, in fact, the desired skills have no actual bearing on effectiveness.[2] The joint RAND–MITRE study found no rigorous, formal studies linking LREC training to individual job performance or unit effectiveness.

In the era of Big Data, one possible approach to the second challenge—that of not knowing which KSAs really matter—is to capture as much information as possible about each candidate on the rationale that *something* must matter to job performance. Doing so still does not address the problem that units might not know what they really need, and it exacerbates the first problem of validity—the more information there is, the more likely that some of it is not just irrelevant but out of date or inaccurate.

The fact that there are challenges to tracking regionally relevant KSAs does not mean that the Army should not try to do so. But consumers of the data must have an understanding of the data's limitations and should not deceive themselves into thinking they know more about job requirements than they really do. The Army as an institution should be wary of codifying regionally relevant KSAs into formal requirements until it has a better understanding of how they support unit effectiveness. Requirements impose real costs on the personnel system as a whole and on soldiers. Every requirement that is added to a billet reduces the number of eligible soldiers, complicates the search process, and increases the likelihood that a position will go unfilled. Worse, if the requirement does not truly enhance mission effectiveness, it might lead to soldiers performing poorly because they were assigned to units on the basis of irrelevant training or experience. Finally, once a new requirement is identified, an extensive set of bureaucratic processes is set in motion. All these issues should be considered carefully before the Army decided to track specific regionally relevant KSAs.

Tracking Regionally Aligned Forces–Relevant Personnel Information

We make a deliberate distinction between *regionally relevant KSAs* and *RAF-relevant personnel information*. KSAs, when considered in an occupational context, should *make some demonstrable contribution to individual performance and organizational effectiveness*. Relevant personnel information is a broader concept that *includes not only KSAs but also things whose connection to individual performance and organizational effectiveness has face validity but is not proven*. At a practical level, the distinction means that

---

[2] An example from the civilian world comes from Teach for America, which has spent more than a decade trying to identify what really makes a difference in teacher effectiveness. At one time, it was believed that teachers would be more effective if they had prior experience working in poor neighborhoods similar to the ones where they would teach. Years of careful study found that similarity of teacher and student backgrounds has no correlation with teacher effectiveness (Ripley, 2010).

what a commander of a regionally aligned unit really wants to know about a soldier is what he or she can do to contribute to mission effectiveness (i.e., KSAs), but, lacking that information, the commander would at least be interested in knowing whether the soldier has already been assigned to another unit aligned with the same region, has an academic degree studying the aligned region, has a spouse from that part of the world, and so forth (i.e., relevant personnel information).

The Army already maintains extensive databases that contain information about the training, education, experience, proficiency, aptitude, and personal background of every soldier. Some of this information might be relevant for regionally aligned units. Examples include prior deployments, assignments to other regionally aligned units, language proficiency, academic degrees in regional studies, and training related to missions, such as security force assistance.

Besides the data resident in official databases, other information about soldiers might be relevant to the RAF concept. For example, the authors of the Green Pages final report wrote that, "according to official Army records (TAPDB), the collective cultural fluency of all pilot effort participants spanned roughly 28 percent of the world. Green Pages revealed, however, that those same officers actually possess cultural fluencies spanning 72% of the world" (OEMA, 2012). The number of languages officers reported being able to speak was roughly double the cumulative number of languages listed in TAPDB for that same group. Yet the authors never define *cultural fluency* or explain how it is inferred from soldiers' personnel data, so it is not clear how it might affect individual performance or unit effectiveness.[3]

Evaluation reports have sections for duty descriptions (distinct from the performance evaluation sections) that could provide useful details about soldiers' actual work experience, above and beyond duty titles and basic unit and deployment information. Using this information to build an experience profile for each person has several advantages. First, it is already organic to the personnel management system—collecting this information does not impose a new system or process on the force. Second, the rater and rated soldier together validate the information, in theory at least, so other units and the soldiers' career managers can be relatively confident in the accuracy. And third, the information comes with supporting metadata, such as duty dates, location, and grade and duty title of the soldier when performing the duties, so its relevance and timeliness are apparent. Although this would be a legitimate and reasonable reuse of existing data, setting up a system that would collect, clean,[4] summarize, and disseminate the data in a useful way would not be trivial.

---

[3] The authors use the phrase "language and cultural fluency" several times, so they presumably do not consider cultural fluency to be synonymous with linguistic fluency.

[4] Cleaning the data would include eliminating any misplaced commentary on a soldier's performance that ended up in the duty-description section. The goal would be to simply identify what the soldier did, not how well the soldier did it.

RAF-relevant personnel data might be objective or subjective; quantitative, categorical, or qualitative; and coded, standardized, or unstructured. The information might exist in comprehensive databases of record, such as TAPDB, or in niche systems, such as Army Career Tracker or Army Green Pages. Data might be found directly in personnel records or might be constructed from a combination of information about a soldier (such as unit assignments) and information about a unit (such as deployment and mission). And the data might be more or less complete, accurate, detailed, current, and relevant to RAF.

But, for the discussion at hand, *the most important distinction is between data that are essential to formal requirements, classification, and structure and those that are not.* Nonessential data do not impose the same costs but can still inform personnel processes and might even provide insights about work and workforce that could eventually lead to formal changes in requirements, classification, training, assignments, and so forth. In our judgment, most RAF-relevant personnel data are still nonessential today because it is too early to know how they support mission effectiveness.

Personnel Development Skill Identifiers: A Low-Cost, Low-Regret Way Ahead

As discussed in the foregoing section, most of the data that might be relevant to assignment decisions are not essential to it. It is premature to determine which skills are essential for regional assignments and which are not. This uncertainty means that the Army should prefer low-cost, low-regret options for tracking RAF-relevant KSAOs. PDSI codes are such an option. They appear to be the most appropriate way to measure and track potentially useful, but currently nonessential, RAF-relevant personnel data. According to DA PAM 611-21, *Military Occupational Classification and Structure,*

> PDSI codes are used, in combination with an AOC [area of concentration]/MOS [military occupational specialty], to identify unique skills, training and/or experience officers, warrants, and enlisted Soldiers may obtain during their careers that could add value to the Army and organization in its mission but do not meet minimum standards for establishment of an ASI [additional skill identifier] . . . can't be coded in authorization documents through identification of standard positions . . . or for other reasons. (U.S. Army, undated [b], ¶ 1-15[a])[5]

In other words, PDSI codes are easier to use than other ways of coding military knowledge and skill, mostly because they can be used to indicate KSAs for which no formal

---

[5]   DA PAM 611-21 is an Army Smartbook, so the Army updates it electronically as changes occur to ensure that all guidance is current. It is maintained as an electronic resource. All citations of DA PAM 611-21 in this document were current as of June 30, 2015.

requirement exists. ASIs, for example, are tied to specific positions in requirements and authorization documents, are used primarily to identify skills that are obtained through formal schooling or civilian certification, and are closely related to MOSs. In other words, the Army must formally determine that there is a need for a specific KSAO and validate the path by which it is attained before establishing, and therefore using, an ASI.[6] Special qualification identifiers (SQIs) are even more restrictive than ASIs in their application and create, in essence, a distinct MOS when combined with a basic four-character MOS code. Like ASIs, SQIs are documented requirements in modified-table-of-organization-and-equipment and table-of-distribution-and-allowance documents. Table 5.1 summarizes the requirements for the various occupational identifiers for military personnel.

Even without creating new PDSIs, the Army can use some existing ones to begin to track and measure RAF-relevant KSAs. Table 5.2 lists several existing PDSIs pulled from the current DA PAM 611-21 (U.S. Army, undated [b]). These PDSIs are earned in a variety of ways: through certifications, university course credit, testing, operational experience, training, and deployment. Some require a combination of criteria, while others require only one; some differentiate by levels of proficiency or skill, while others are binary; some are restricted to certain CMFs, while others are open to all. In short, even this small sample of PDSIs—there are nearly 100 total—shows the flexibility in how PDSIs are constructed and what they measure.

Perhaps the simplest approach for creating new PDSIs that track RAF-relevant KSAs is to base them on assignments to regionally aligned units. This is the same metric we used for our analysis of potential breadth and depth of regional experience, described in Chapter Four. A more-nuanced variation would be to measure different levels of experience using cumulative time assigned to regionally aligned units and operational deployments. Existing PDSIs, such as D5E and D5F (intermediate- and advanced-level language skills) and T2C and T2D (AFPAK Hands intermediate language skill and AFPAK Hands advanced deployment skill), incorporate experience and deployments into graded PDSI levels. Such an approach would likely require separate PDSIs for each region of the world with which a unit can be aligned. This assignment- or deployment-based approach could result in the notional PDSIs listed in Table 5.3.

It is necessary to track experience formally for two reasons. First, the assignment history on a Soldier Record Brief (SRB) cannot clearly indicate alignment in and of itself. Most units will be based in the continental United States, so it will not be possible to infer alignment from information about duty station. Moreover, as of this writing, the Army intends to vary units' alignment with various regions over time (Vergun, 2013). This practice complicates tracking soldiers' accrual of regional experi-

---

[6] Not all of these characteristics apply to Professional Development Proficiency Codes, which are a special and uncommon type of ASI. Still, Professional Development Proficiency Codes are not used in the same way that PDSIs are and are not as appropriate for tracking RAF-relevant KSAs.

Table 5.1
Minimum Requirements for Occupational Identifiers

Category	Personnel	Minimum Number of Positions	Formal Training	Review Every Two Years	Reference	Other
Commissioned officer						
AOC	Yes	40	Yes; branch-, AOC-, or FA-specific requirement	No	DA PAM 611-21 ¶¶ 2-2 and 2-6	Different from an existing AOC. Peculiar to one branch or FA.
Skill identifier	Yes	20	Yes; 2 weeks formal or equivalent	Yes	DA PAM 611-21 ¶ 2-6	Does not duplicate AOC duties. Clear advantage derived.
WO						
MOS	Yes	35	Yes; MOS-specific requirements	No	DA PAM 611-21 ¶ 6-29	Continuous application of unique aptitudes, talents, and abilities. High degree of technical or tactical skills not readily available within commissioned or enlisted structure. Based on operational requirement and maintenance for combat readiness.
SQI	Yes	10	No; 2 weeks formal or 6 months OJT or OJE	Yes	DA PAM 611-21 ¶ 6-29	Does not require all WOs in an MOS to perform. Clear advantage derived.
ASI	Yes	10	Yes; 2 weeks formal or equivalent	Yes	DA PAM 611-21 ¶ 6-29	Does not require all WOs in an MOS to perform. Clear advantage derived.
Enlisted soldier						
MOS	Yes	75	Yes; MOS-specific requirement	No	DA PAM 611-21 ¶ 9-4	Identify types of skills without regard to levels. Duty positions with closely related skills.

Table 5.1—Continued

Category	Personnel	Minimum Number of Positions	Formal Training	Review Every Two Years	Reference	Other
SQI	Yes	20	No; formal training or 6 months OJT or OJE	Yes	DA PAM 611-21 ¶ 9-7	Requirements do not change with MOS association. Not an MOS substitute or the sole skill required.
ASI	Yes	20 each MOS	Yes; 10 days	Yes	DA PAM 611-21 ¶ 9-8	Requirements do not change with MOS association. Not an MOS substitute or the sole skill required. Must not be awarded only from OJT or OJE.
PDSI						
PDSI	Yes	None	No	Yes	DA PAM 611-21 Chapters 1, 2, 6, and 9	Used with all grades to identify the type of knowledge or expertise soldiers have acquired in projects, systems, concepts, or items of equipment under development, testing, or implementation for which an occupational identifier has not been created.

SOURCE: U.S. Army, undated (b), Table 1-8.

NOTE: FA = functional area. OJT = on-the-job training. OJE = on-the-job experience.

Table 5.2
Existing Regionally Aligned Forces–Relevant Personnel Development Skill Identifiers

PDSI	Title	Qualification
C4A	Overseas contingency operations planning	Certificate in overseas contingency operations planning from the U.S. Army Command and General Staff College
D4P	Military observer, peacekeeping operations	• Predeployment training course administered by U.S. Military Observers Group, Washington, and • 6-month deployment in support of United Nations peacekeeping operations
D5E	Intermediate-level language skills	• 2/2 on oral proficiency interview and • USAJFKSWCS intermediate or advanced regional studies course or 6 credit hours in cultural studies from an accredited university • Restricted to CMFs 18, 37, and 38
D5F	Advanced-level language skills	• 3/3 on oral proficiency interview and • USAJFKSWCS intermediate or advanced regional studies course or 6 credit hours in cultural studies from an accredited university and • Minimum 2 years operational experience and 2 deployments in the AOR of the assigned language at SOF tactical element level • Restricted to CMFs 18, 37, and 38
D5K	Cultural support team	Cultural support team course, phases 1 and 2, at USAJFKSWCS
T1D	Training and transition team, 162nd-trained	Training and transition team training conducted by the 162nd Infantry Training Brigade, Fort Polk, Louisiana, mobile training team
T2C	AFPAK Hands intermediate language skill	Advanced language training, counterinsurgency, and culture training and all requirements for AFPAK Hands initial deployment skill
T2D	AFPAK Hands advanced deployment skill	1-year deployment to Afghanistan or Pakistan in AFPAK Hands joint manning document billet

SOURCE: U.S. Army, undated (b).

NOTE: USAJFKSWCS = U.S. Army John F. Kennedy Special Warfare Center and School. CMF 18 = special forces. CMF 37 = psychological operations. CMF 38 = civil affairs.

Table 5.3
Notional New Personnel Development Skill Identifiers for Regionally Aligned Forces

PDSI	Title	Qualification
T4A	Initial AFRICOM alignment	Minimum 24 months assigned to units regionally aligned with AFRICOM
T4B	Intermediate AFRICOM alignment	• Minimum 36 months assigned to units regionally aligned with AFRICOM and • 1 deployment, any length, to the AFRICOM AOR
T4C	Advanced AFRICOM alignment	• Minimum 48 months assigned to units regionally aligned with AFRICOM and • Minimum 12 months deployed to the AFRICOM AOR

NOTE: Other regions would have similar titles and qualifications.

ence. Without cross-checking against a history of alignments, personnel managers will not be able to know the region with which a soldier's unit was aligned at the time the soldier was assigned to it. Second, the Army might wish to add criteria to the PDSI as indicated above, either specifying actual operational deployments or deployments of a certain length. PDSIs should not be awarded solely on the basis of military experience and education, however, but should rather accommodate a wide range of education and experiences.

Obviously, alignment does not equate to experience, and experiences vary in terms of their contribution to expertise. A soldier in a regionally aligned unit might or might not deploy. If he or she does, the soldier's experience might or might not provide meaningful experience in a region's operationally relevant dynamics. A soldier on a military training team accrues considerable experience dealing with partners; a soldier manning a watchtower at Camp Lemonnier in Djibouti does not. Both soldiers might, however, acquire useful experience in synthetic training environments tailored for the operational environment.

Regional expertise can come from many different sources. Any system of tracking and measuring RAF education and experience must accommodate such different sources, which can include soldiers' ethnic heritage, details of their education experiences and civilian experiences on religious missions or work with other nongovernmental organizations, or research and writing on topics relevant to particular regions. Moreover, the problem the Army currently faces is that personnel managers have no visibility into soldiers' regional expertise. At this point, it is probably better for the Army to accept risk of overclassifying soldiers as having regional experience than underclassify them. Over time, the Army can refine its criteria.

The 2009 Army Culture and Foreign Language Strategy (ACFLS) identifies two categories of soldiers with LREC skills: *culture professionals* and *culture generalists*. A culture professional, according to the strategy, is a soldier with "a highly advanced level of knowledge, skills, and attributes that pertain to the culture of a particular country or region of the world. . . . This category of individuals requires some degree of proficiency in a foreign language" (U.S. Army, 2009, p. 18). A culture generalist "possesses a sufficient level of cross-cultural competence and regional competence to effectively accomplish duties at [his or her] assigned level. . . . This category would include most of the leaders and Soldiers in the general force" (U.S. Army, 2009, p. 19).

Assigning PDSIs to soldiers based on their unit assignments and deployments would identify culture generalists. But perhaps what is really important is tracking soldiers in the specific FAs and MOSs where the culture professionals are to be found, such as SOF, foreign area officers, and various intelligence MOSs, as envisioned in the ACFLS. In that case, the PDSI qualifications might closely resemble those of D5E and D5F (intermediate- and advanced-level language skills) in Table 5.2: a combination of operational experience and language skill and restricted by CMF.

One caution about using assignments and deployments as the basis for PDSI codes is that there is an implicit assumption that experience confers some knowledge or skill related to the region with which a soldier's unit is aligned. If the PDSI qualifications are constructed as in Table 5.3, they further assume that more experience confers greater knowledge or skill. These are not unreasonable assumptions, but they embody a very different approach from one that requires some demonstration of skill through proficiency testing, or even completion of a specific training course. On the other hand, because the ACFLS was never fully implemented,[7] it would be speculative right now to declare what proficiency tests (other than language) or RAF-related training, aside from mission-related collective training, the Army wants to track.

One potential approach would be to institute a system for awarding PDSIs that resembles the experiential path in the joint qualification system. In that system, officers apply for experiential joint-duty credit based on the nature of their duties (what they do) and their work environment (with whom they do it) (DoD, 2013). Similarly, the Army could adopt broad criteria for awarding regional qualification PDSIs and delegate specific judgments to a board at HRC. Alternatively, that function could simply be delegated to assignment officers and career managers.

There is a very practical limitation to using PDSIs to track RAF-relevant KSAs. Specifically, the Army's current process for managing PDSIs is not automated: Soldiers' qualifications are individually reviewed and then the codes are manually entered into the TAPDB within G-1. The process as currently configured probably is incapable of handling large batches of updates as soldiers rotate out of units and return from deployments.

We have at least anecdotal evidence that minimal attention is paid to PDSIs, by either assignment officers or the officers they are managing. The codes are difficult to find in the Total Officer Personnel Management Information System (they are "hidden," according to one former desk officer at HRC), and the codes do not appear on Officer Record Briefs. The Enlisted Record Brief does have a field for a single PDSI and date, but a soldier can acquire multiple PDSIs over the course of a career, so it is possible that not all would appear on an Enlisted Record Brief. Moreover, PDSIs are not reported through the Electronic Military Personnel Office system, according to DA PAM 611-21 (U.S. Army, undated [b]). The coming SRB, to be deployed under the Integrated Personnel and Pay System—Army, includes a field for PDSIs, but again, how they will be prioritized for reporting is unclear. But even if all of a soldier's PDSIs are evident on a form, people will not be able to understand them without a data dictionary. The real key for usability is that they be searchable in an electronic database, not that they be printed on a form.

---

[7] This is according to Army Leader Development Program, 2014, to accompany the August 12, 2014, Army Leader Development Forum. The same document noted that not only has the ACFLS not been implemented but funding for implementation is not funded beyond fiscal year 2014. See pp. 8 and 28 in that report for more detail.

Despite these philosophical and practical limitations, using PDSI codes to track RAF-related experience seems a reasonable first step toward a mature personnel management system that fully embraces and supports the RAF concept. PDSI codes have flexibility in how they are constructed but do not impose additional requirements on the assignment and personnel management system. They can be selectively applied to certain grades or CMFs as an initial workaround for the largely manual process by which they are current managed. Their implied correlation of KSAs with experience is not unreasonable. And they establish a modicum of standardization that can give the Army a basis for analyzing and understanding the true value of RAF-related experience and KSAs.

Longer-Term Possibilities for Tracking and Measuring Knowledge, Skills, and Abilities

The last point about analyzing and understanding the true value of RAF-related experience and KSAs is a critical one. New methods and algorithms are emerging under a constellation of terms, such as *analytics*, *business intelligence*, *network analysis*, *Web 2.0*, and the latest—*Big Data*—that are centered on the idea of observing how people use data and tools that are available to them on customized systems. The Army's OEMA analyzed how personnel managers and individual officers used the information provided in Green Pages. The Person–Event Data Environment, hosted by the Army Analytics Group, is another organization that can conduct such analyses or enable others to do so using the vast data sets it houses.

Establishing a standardized way of tracking and measuring RAF-relevant experience, one that is easy to communicate and comprehend, is part of a process of learning which regionally relevant KSAs are truly relevant for individual performance and unit effectiveness, in what contexts, and for which soldiers. The structure that comes with PDSIs can complement large amounts of unstructured data available in myriad places. One potentially rich source of unstructured data is the duty description section in evaluation reports, which are now machine-readable, meaning that they are also searchable and available for other, more-sophisticated processing and analysis. This can provide a very useful record of soldiers' experience and can shed light on their KSAs, whether RAF-relevant or otherwise. Other niche or developmental systems, such as the Army Green Pages and Army Career Tracker, contain additional unstructured data. All of this can be linked to additional information collected through Center for Army Lessons Learned reports and other narratives, interviews, evaluations of training events, and so forth.

Mission requirements will arise faster than the formal military occupational classification structure can respond. The level of detail that units seek will often be greater than what standard databases can provide. Technology will increasingly enable decentralized search and management of soldiers' KSAs and experience, whether RAF-related or otherwise.

Conclusions

To summarize, **we recommend using PDSIs as a low-regret, low-cost means of providing assignment managers and units with basic, structured, standardized information about soldiers' RAF-relevant experience.** As Army implementation of the ACFLS matures, or other LREC-related professional development initiatives come to fruition, it might be appropriate to design PDSIs with qualifications that align with those efforts. Because of the limitations in how PDSIs are managed today, it might be necessary at the outset to limit awarding PDSIs only to soldiers in certain grades or CMFs.

Today's problem, however, is that Army personnel managers have minimal visibility into soldiers' regional experience and education. Formal overseas deployments and language proficiency appear on SRBs, if the soldiers in question have maintained those records. Other relevant educational coursework, background (e.g., study abroad), and experience are more or less invisible. **Ergo, the Army should establish broad, inclusive criteria for awarding region-oriented PDSIs based on education and experience.** PDSIs should do the following:

- Identify the combatant commands with which soldiers are aligned by virtue of some combination of education and experience.
- Vary according to soldiers' levels of education and experience. Personnel managers should be able to distinguish between soldiers who merely have been aligned and those who have deployed and between those who have deployed once and those who have deployed several times.
- Err on the side of inclusion because it is unclear what kinds and levels of formal education, self-study, and operational experience contribute to regional expertise.

As time goes by, the Army should implement processes to assess how the PDSIs and other, less-structured data identify information about soldiers that ultimately correlates with individual performance and unit effectiveness. As we discuss in the next chapter, the Army's adoption of talent management—in which market mechanisms enable personnel managers to better align individual talents with specific jobs' requirements—provides a useful venue for doing so. Talent management provides Army officials with the opportunity to differentiate those skills that are truly useful to stakeholders from those that only seem to be.

CHAPTER SIX

Findings and Recommendations

Findings

RAF represents a significant change in direction for the U.S. Army as it responds to changes in the U.S. defense strategy. As such, it is appropriate that the Army adapt its personnel system to support RAF. Given RAF's relatively nascent state, however, its precise implications for Army personnel policy and practice remain unclear, though its requirements are likely to remain relatively modest. It is therefore appropriate to undertake only low-cost, low-regret measures at this time to support RAF. Highlighting soldiers' regional education and experience levels using PDSIs and using that information to support assignment decisions under a talent management approach—to which the Army is already committed—should suffice to enable the Army to meet operational units' needs for regional expertise.

The Army's RAF initiative represents one aspect of its response to evolving U.S. strategy that is shifting away from direct engagement to counter instability and from deterring adversaries to enabling partners and allies to do so. Instead of deploying as whole units within the framework of large-scale counterinsurgency operations, Army forces will find themselves deploying in smaller, more-tailored packages to a wider variety of operational environments. Instead of directing operations, headquarters elements will increasingly focus on identifying and exploiting opportunities to shape the security environment, work for partners, and reduce the sphere of instability.

As the Army adapts to support U.S. strategy, it is important for its personnel policy to evolve as well. The Army wishes to enhance units' familiarity with and expertise regarding areas in which they are likely to be employed. Beyond competence in region-specific languages and culture, it is possible to imagine additional KSAOs that might be needed in particular regional contexts. These competencies and their development mean that the successful execution of RAF will affect and be affected by the balance of breadth and depth of Army leaders' operational experience.

However, the Army's ability to identify and track such KSAOs throughout soldiers' careers is limited. Regional alignment thus appears to have potential implications for leader development and personnel management, but the magnitude and direction of these implications have yet to be identified.

The Army Has Relatively Little Empirical Information About the Personnel Implications of Regionally Aligned Forces

The Army's experience with RAF to date has been too limited to indicate a clear direction for Army personnel management. Relatively few units have deployed and conducted operations under RAF. As of this writing, elements of only about four of the Army's current 38 BCTs, and a similarly low proportion of its enablers, have deployed under RAF. Employment has differed significantly within each combatant command's AOR. Forces deploying to AFRICOM have done so mostly in small elements, largely to train, advise, and assist African security forces in peacekeeping and stability operations. Forces deploying to Europe, in contrast, have done so in organized units in the context of increased emphasis on conventional deterrence. USARPAC's Pacific Pathways effort falls somewhere in between. Moreover, the Army has yet to conduct a rigorous assessment of these diverse operations, probably because the size of the potential sample remains too small.

To be sure, there are many similarities between the Army's recent experience with counterinsurgency and its RAF mission, particularly the importance of understanding the operational environment and the need to develop partners' capability and capacity. The differences between recent experience and the kind of employment envisaged under RAF might outweigh the similarities, however. Perhaps the critical distinction is that the mission of working with partners was secondary to conducting or supporting U.S. combat operations for most Army forces in Iraq and Afghanistan. Closely related is the fact that unit efforts took place in the context of immense infrastructures devoted to developing partner capabilities in both countries. Ergo, Army forces' experiences in Iraq and Afghanistan suggest useful directions for adaptation but are not dispositive.

It is thus impossible to say that historical experience under RAF or in the Army's recent history clearly demonstrates the efficacy of any particular adaptation of the Army's personnel system. Saying that history indicates no clear and unambiguous direction for the personnel system is by no means the same thing as saying that history shows that there is no need for change. It is probably more accurate to say that the empirical evidence available indicates a need for change but cannot yet indicate the nature and extent of the required changes in a clear and comprehensive fashion.

Potential Demand for Regional Expertise Appears Likely to Be Moderate at This Time

The available information is probably sufficient to estimate the potential scope and scale of the requirement for regional expertise in support of RAF. Limited experience under RAF to date indicates that extensive prior experience and education are not essential for the satisfactory conduct of training and advisory missions at the tactical level. Moreover, pre-mission training conducted in units seems to prepare units adequately for those missions, whether those missions involve training African forces in peacekeeping or rehearsing conventional combat operations in Europe. Note that it is impossible to say whether this degree of preparation is optimal or merely satisfactory. All that can be said with some degree of confidence is that Army forces have yet to fail unambiguously in their missions. In the absence of such failure, however, there are as yet no indications that the Army *must* adapt its personnel policies to enable RAF units' tactical success.

There is probably a need to enhance regional expertise at operational echelons responsible for shaping conditions for the tactical employment of RAF units. Operational echelons include headquarters at the division level[1] and higher and theater-level enablers, such as theater sustainment commands, theater intelligence brigades, and theater signal brigades. An expert panel convened by the study team recommended that the Army designate key billets in such organizations for fill with soldiers with prior regional experience. The panel considered that prior experience was particularly important for soldiers in military intelligence, signal, and logistics career management fields. Such experience and, by extension, expertise were considered important because soldiers at this level were responsible for responding to the unique requirements of the theater. For example, operational sustainment across the Pacific's vast distances and its nations' irregular levels of economic development differs significantly from that in conditions in Europe. Moreover, panelists and others we interviewed considered the development of relationships with partners essential to identifying and leveraging opportunities for military engagement. As discussed at greater length in Chapter Three, the total number of billets requiring some degree of regional expertise probably does not exceed 4,300.

As with any other conclusion about the future direction of the RAF initiative, this finding rests on very limited empirical data. Our expert panel's collective experience in the kinds of operational environments envisioned under RAF is likewise limited. As the Army acquires additional experience with RAF, this estimate should be reviewed and might be subject to revision.

Acquiring Regional Expertise Need Not Conflict with Traditional Career Development Patterns

Fortunately, acquiring regional expertise need not come at the expense of acquiring functional expertise. Regional expertise is a function of education and experience in the application of military functional skills in a particular regional context. A system requiring regional expertise might well differ from current policies and practices in channeling soldiers into key and developmental assignments in a single region, rather than potentially across many regions. In effect, soldiers would continue to follow existing career models.

---

[1]   Division and corps are often considered tactical headquarters in the context of major operations. When configured as JTFs, however, such headquarters can have operational-level responsibilities. Examples include the attempt to organize U.S. stabilization and reconstruction efforts in Iraq under Combined JTF 7 in Iraq in 2003–2004 and U.S. operations in Haiti under the XVIII Airborne Corps.

The Army Will Probably Produce Enough Soldiers with Relevant Expertise to Meet This Modest Demand

Normal assignment practices will probably produce enough soldiers with the requisite experience to meet this limited demand for expertise, at least as long as the Army maintains approximately the same end strength and posture. In general, our analysis indicated that there would be enough soldiers with multiple tours in each region to meet each region's demand for expertise and a larger pool of soldiers with at least one tour available for that purpose. This analysis assumes some degree of formal education in regional issues to combine with experience. Moreover, the Army almost surely has many soldiers with relevant expertise of whom it is currently unaware because it has no means of capturing and sharing the information. It must be acknowledged that the requirement for prior regional experience lies in tension with other requirements and would probably limit the inventory of soldiers available to fill those key billets to some degree. We must further acknowledge that it will take some time to develop a distribution of regional expertise similar to the one we simulated because most soldiers' actual formative experiences have been overwhelmingly in the CENTCOM AOR.

Current Personnel Management Practices and Systems Do Not Enable the Army to Match Supply with Demand

Two major problems remain: validating the positions that actually require regional expertise and matching soldiers with the required expertise to those positions. Although insights from RAF practitioners and our panel provide a sufficient basis to assess the approximate scope and scale of the requirement for regional expertise, that estimate cannot serve as the basis for specific assignments. Instead, using commands would have to validate the positions that either require or would benefit from specific regional expertise. Doing so would require comparing the performance of soldiers with such expertise and that of soldiers who lack it.

Making this comparison is especially difficult because soldiers' previous regional experience is largely invisible to personnel managers, however. The records actually used to assign soldiers indicate the units with which soldiers have served but not their regional alignment at the time of assignment. Personnel records indicate educational qualifications only in general terms. For example, a soldier's record might indicate civilian school and major but omit any regional dimensions to that major or coursework. Military education records indicate only the school attended and contain no information about coursework in regional subjects. The records most commonly used by personnel managers convey relatively little information about regionally relevant education and experience. In short, unless personnel managers personally know the soldiers they are managing, they will have a hard time assessing those soldiers' levels of regional expertise.

Recommendations

Leverage the Army's Adoption of Talent Management

Given the low level of experience with RAF and the concomitantly high level of uncertainty about what it requires, the Army should adapt its personnel system to support RAF incrementally. The Army should mostly undertake measures that promise benefits no matter what is learned from RAF implementation or at least minimize costs. For example, the Army should not remake its entire personnel system to support RAF based on the limited information available today.

On the other hand, the Army is adopting a personnel management approach of talent management, starting with its senior leaders (McHugh and Odierno, 2014; Colarusso and Lyle, 2014). Talent management can support RAF, as well as many other imperatives. Talent management is a broad and often ill-defined subject. In this context, it involves matching soldiers to positions based on the soldiers' unique competencies and positions' specific requirements. It contrasts with the current military personnel system that assigns soldiers based simply on CMF and grade. Army analysts have already identified talent management as being critical to RAF's implementation (Bukowski et al., 2014).

Leveraging talent management would enable the Army to learn which billets require what degree of regional expertise from experience, rather than trying to guess correctly in advance. Commands and units could indicate the positions they believe require regional expertise and the degree of education and experience required. As discussed earlier, most positions will probably require no significant amount of prior regional experience or education. Assignment officers and assignment managers can then nominate soldiers who best meet the various criteria—regional and otherwise—to fill those positions. By observing and analyzing this process over time, the Army can identify which positions require some degree of regional expertise and then adapt education, training, and career development models to provide soldiers with the required expertise more efficiently.

Make Information About Soldiers' Regionally Aligned Forces–Relevant Education and Experience Available to Personnel Managers

A talent management approach requires relevant information to function effectively. As indicated earlier, Army personnel managers lack information about soldiers' RAF-relevant education and experience. In this analysis, we have focused on the issue of regionally relevant military experience; soldiers' personal experience and education are also relevant. The Army should provide those data.

PDSIs provide a ready-made vehicle for doing so. The Army already uses PDSIs to track certain key skills gained through experience or OJT, such as digital training. PDSIs differ from other kinds of skill identifiers in that they track soldier attributes but do not constitute requirements that must be met in order to fill individual billets. In other words, PDSIs provide information that is useful to but not binding on personnel managers. The Army could use PDSIs to track formal education, training, and experience related to particular regions and to convey that information to personnel managers at the Army and unit levels. The Army could use a variety of criteria for awarding PDSIs, including not only military education and experience but also that obtained from civilian education, self-study, and civilian background. Requesting units could use them to identify the kind and amount of education and experience desired for different positions.

Although PDSIs exist, they are largely invisible to personnel managers under the current system. The SRB, to be deployed under the Integrated Personnel and Pay System—Army, includes a field for PDSIs. Although a soldier can acquire many PDSIs over the course of a career, the Army could prioritize RAF-relevant information for inclusion in this field on the SRB.

Allow a Regional Qualification System to Evolve

In the course of this study, a panel of Army and RAND experts concluded that a regional qualification system, in which certain key billets would be reserved for soldiers with appropriate levels of regional expertise, would best mitigate risks and exploit opportunities inherent in personnel management in support of RAF implementation. The panel determined that the kinds of positions that might require regional expertise existed mostly at operational echelons. Those echelons include JTF-capable division and corps headquarters and operational enablers, such as theater sustainment commands, theater intelligence brigades, and strategic signal brigades. Positions tentatively included staff principals, planners, and technical experts with theater-level responsibilities.

Neither the panel nor any other participant in this study had the opportunity to identify specific billets requiring such regional expertise in any sort of analytically rigorous fashion. Even if they had had such opportunity, they have relatively little empirical experience on which to base such analysis. Certainly, operations in Iraq and Afghanistan have highlighted the importance of language, culture, and other regional aspects of the operational environments. Yet, just as there are geographical differences between recent theaters of operation and the wider scope of operational environments envisioned under RAF, so too are there differences in the range of military operations to be conducted and their intensity. Attempting to identify specific billets in advance thus incurs significant risk of identifying the wrong ones.

Fortunately, it is unnecessary to do so. If soldiers' regional expertise does contribute significantly to success in certain billets, one would expect to observe soldiers with such expertise to be selected for such jobs at significantly higher rates than soldiers who lack such expertise under a talent management system. Army personnel managers should thus analyze assignment decisions made in this context over time in order to determine which positions benefit from regional expertise and which do not. Results might well differ depending on the region.

For Further Study

At least three areas remain for further study: increasing utilization of foreign area officers (FAOs) under RAF, recruiting and retaining heritage speakers of key languages,[2] and developing senior leaders' regional expertise. These three areas represent different approaches to increasing levels of regional expertise available to Army forces. Obviously, the former two issues concern integrating higher levels of regional expertise into the planning and conduct of military operations. RAF's cognitive challenge, however, lies in integrating operational and regional expertise to optimize capabilities for particular operational environments. FAOs' operational experience, and hence expertise, lies primarily at lower tactical levels, however. Heritage speakers have even less military experience. Intuitively, it seems that the Army would benefit from improving operational experts' regional expertise and improving regional experts' operational expertise, but the precise combination of these two initiatives requires further study. Developing senior leaders' levels of regional expertise warrants additional on the basis of their importance to the success of Army forces and to achieving national objectives.

Increasing Utilization of Foreign Area Officers

This analysis has focused mostly on the degree to which the Army should increase soldiers' regional expertise in order to optimize unit performance in the regional contexts envisioned under RAF. Examples include understanding how the AOR's military geography constrains operational maneuver or how the state of the region's economies and infrastructure enables operational logistics. Another option for adapting RAF units to specific operational environments might include adapting FAOs' roles and increasing their number. FAOs are currently the Army's repository of regional expertise. Per DA PAM 600-3, FAOs are to possess particular competency in "cross-cultural capabilities, interpersonal communications, language skills, interagency integration and regional political–military expertise" (U.S. Army, 2014b, p. 277). They are particularly concerned with the mechanics of security assistance and mostly—though by no means exclusively—employed at the strategic level, informing diplomatic leaders about military capabilities and strategy and advising military leaders about the political constraints and limitations involved in operating in a particular country.

Yet, although most soldiers might need to increase their levels of regional expertise under RAF, FAOs might need to improve their levels of operational expertise.

---

[2] Heritage speakers are generally either immigrants themselves or the children of immigrants and thus presumably also understand the cultures that go along with those languages fairly well.

As LTC Daniel Mouton points out, "most officers recruited into the FAO program lack operational experience following company-level command at around the eighth year of service" (Mouton, 2011, p. 21). Most of these officers are assigned to embassies, strategic-level headquarters, or the institutional Army. Employing them more frequently in support of military engagement missions might require increasing the number of FAO billets as well.

Recruiting and Retaining Heritage Speakers

The Army might also be able to increase its reservoir of regional expertise by recruiting more heritage speakers of key languages. The Army's translator/linguist (09L) program and its Military Accessions Vital to the National Interest program provide templates for this sort of initiative. Regional expertise appears to be most important at operational echelons, at which first-term soldiers seldom play significant roles. The success of such initiatives would therefore hinge on heritage speakers' propensity to serve beyond their initial obligations.

Developing Senior Leaders' Regional Expertise

RAF is focused on Army units and improving their capabilities to operate in a regional context. Organized units—including theater armies, corps, and divisions—generally operate at the operational or tactical level of war. The panel thus did not explicitly consider the impact that alternative personnel management concepts could have on the Army's ability to develop leaders who can engage at strategic levels. Clearly, however, developing such leaders is important to the Army and to the joint force as regional considerations loom larger in the formulation and execution of U.S. strategy. Several of those we interviewed stressed the importance of developing and employing senior leaders' regional expertise and relationships with officials in partner nations. Other functions and issues have a regional dimension as well, including resource allocation in the context of DoD's planning, programming, budgeting, and execution system; human resource management; and defense strategy formulation and evaluation. Given the decisive importance of senior leaders to the Army and to effective functioning in these areas, the Army should therefore explore this topic further.

Conclusion

Clearly, the Army should continue to adapt its personnel system to evolving operational demands. The RAF concept affects the nature of those operational demands and thus implies some change for the Army personnel system. The extremely limited empirical information available to date seems to point to some sort of regional qualification system, in which prior regional education and experience will serve as prerequisites for selection to certain key billets.

Our analysis indicates that the Army will probably develop enough soldiers with the requisite expertise to meet the demands that a regional qualification might impose, at least as long as it maintains approximately the same end strength and force posture. The problem lies in identifying the billets that require such expertise and matching the right soldiers to those billets. There is a risk, however, that attempting to identify billets and specific requirements based on information now available will lead to error later. The Army's current practice of rotating units' alignment among regions further complicates matters because unit requirements for regional expertise will continually change.

Talent management addresses the problem and its accompanying risk, allowing for the Army's internal labor market to identify both the billets that require expertise and the nature of the expertise needed to fill them. The key to this approach is providing personnel managers with information about soldiers' RAF-relevant education and experience and enabling them to make decisions based on that information.

Methods, Analysis, and Results of the Expert Panel

We convened a panel of 12 experts[1] to evaluate the three RAF concepts: the current concept or baseline, RDA, and RCA. This appendix presents the methods, analysis, and results of the expert panel elicitation.

Methods

The expert panel elicitation followed the Delphi method (e.g., Ayyub, 2001; Brown, 1968; Sackman, 1974). The Delphi method is a structured group elicitation technique in which participants are surveyed about the topic under consideration in two or more rounds. Between the first and second rounds, participants are provided with a summary of anonymous survey results. The group members might discuss this summary, providing their reasoning for survey answers. In the second round, participants are encouraged to revise their answers to the survey based on the summary and group discussion.

Prior to convening the expert panel, we provided participants with supporting materials, including a description of the different personnel concepts and the operational and personnel management objectives. During round 1 of the expert panel's discussion, we asked participants to assess the current personnel system's capability with respect to the identified objectives. This established a baseline capability for each risk objective. With those baseline capabilities in mind, participants were then asked to assess three different probabilities: that alternatives would improve, maintain, or degrade that capability. Finally, we asked participants to assess each objective's importance to the Army's overall objectives. These elicited values allowed for an analysis of the overall expected value of each alternative, as discussed further in the next section.

Subsequent to round 1, we presented the panel with a summary analysis of survey results, and panel members discussed the assessments with regard to the two major objectives: operational risk and personnel management risks. In round 2, we gave par-

---

[1] A representative from the sponsoring organization also participated, but we excluded his assessments from the analysis so as not to bias the results.

ticipants the opportunity to revise their initial assessment based on the discussion and summary analysis.

Analysis

We used participants' assessments to calculate expected values for the personnel RAF concepts. These analyses are based on the concept of utility. In economics, utility represents an individual's preferences over some set of goods and services (von Neumann and Morgenstern, 1947; Savage, 1954). In other words, utility is the quantification of the satisfaction one would get from a certain good or service. Utility theory maintains that, when considering a set of options, a rational individual chooses the option that provides the most utility or value (von Neumann and Morgenstern, 1947; Savage, 1954). The theory is often extended to include options with uncertain outcomes in a theory named *expected utility theory*. Under this theory, an uncertain option can have multiple possible outcomes, each with different expected probabilities of occurrence. The expected utility (or value) for the option is the sum-product of the probability and the utility (value) for each outcome (von Neumann and Morgenstern, 1947; Savage, 1954).[2]

We first calculated the utility, or value, of the baseline by asking participants to assess its capability with respect to the identified objectives on a scale of 1 to 5, demarcated as follows:

- 1 (poor): Army forces will often fail to achieve desired objectives in this mission category because of shortcomings in soldiers' competencies (functional and regional) under the current personnel management system.
- 2 (inadequate): Army forces will fail to achieve desired objectives in this mission category more frequently than necessary because of shortcomings in soldiers' competencies (regional and functional) under the current personnel management system.
- 3 (neutral): The general level of soldiers' competencies (regional and functional) under the current personnel management system neither significantly increases nor decreases the chances of success in this mission category.
- 4 (adequate): Army forces will succeed in this mission category more frequently than might otherwise be expected because of soldiers' general levels of regional and functional competencies.
- 5 (good): Army forces will usually succeed in this mission category because of soldiers' general levels of regional and functional competencies.

---

[2]   Each option includes several components, e.g., risk with respect to regional security cooperation and risk with respect to global contingency operations. Overall risk is the *sum* of the risks of these components. The risk with regard to each component is a *product* of the probability and consequence of that occurrence.

These baseline consequence ratings ($c_{baseline}$) determined the value of an alternative RAF concept maintaining that capability ($v_{maintain}$) as

$$v_{maintain} = \frac{c_{baseline} - 1}{4}.$$

We also set the value of an alternative RAF concept significantly improving that capability to $v_{improve} = 1$ and significantly degrading that capability to $v_{degrade} = 0$.

Next, we calculated the probability of alternatives to significantly improve, maintain, or significantly degrade the level of performance experienced under the baseline with respect to each of the objectives by asking participants to assess the probability on a scale from 1 (not at all likely) to 5 (extremely likely). We converted participants' answers to probabilities, as shown in Table A.1.

The probabilities of an alternative improving ($p_{improve}$), maintaining ($p_{maintain}$), and degrading ($p_{degrade}$) the level of performance experienced under the current system were then normalized ($np_{improve}$, $np_{maintain}$, $np_{degrade}$) such that they would sum to 1.

Using expected utility theory, then, the expected value for risk category i (ev_i) would be the sum-product of the normalized probability and value levels:

$$ev_i = \left(np_{degrade} \times 0 \right) + \left(np_{maintain} \times v_{maintain} \right) + \left(np_{improve} \times 1 \right)$$

for the ith risk category, where $np_{degrade} = np_{improve} = 0$ for the baseline personnel concept.

Expected values for each risk objective can be between 0 (very low value) and 1 (very high value).

Finally, for each RAF alternative, we calculated the weighted average of the expected values to obtain an overall expected value for each alternative. We weighted the expected value for each risk objective by the importance ratings elicited from par-

Table A.1
Conversion of Participant Ratings to Probabilities

Rating	Probability
1 (not at all likely)	0.1
2	0.3
3	0.5
4	0.7
5 (extremely likely)	0.9

ticipants on a scale from 1 (not at all important) to 5 (extremely important). We converted the importance rating (r_i) for each risk category i to weights (w_i) as

$$w_i = \frac{r_i}{\sum\limits_{i=1}^{n} r_i}$$

for a total of n objectives.

Therefore, an overall expected value could be calculated as

$$ev = \sum_{i=1}^{8} ev_i w_i.$$

Overall expected values can be between 0 (very low value) and 1 (very high value).

We handled items that were unanswered as follows: For probability judgments, we set missing values to 1 (very unlikely); for judgments on the capability of the baseline, we set missing values to the midpoint of 3.

Participants

Thirteen soldiers participated in the expert panel. Of those 13 participants, seven served with the Army between 19 and 36 years ($M = 27.7$). These seven participants were deployed on contingency operations or in security cooperation activities between eight and 52 months ($M = 32.9$). Four served as personnel managers for lengths of time between 18 and 36 years ($M = 25.3$).

Results

Interpretation of Results

By eliciting the probability of three different outcomes (that an alternative would improve, maintain, or degrade the level of performance experienced by the current system), our analysis essentially elicited a probability density function for each RAF alternative. To reduce the burden on our participants, we elicited these functions in their most simplified form. However, the approach also reduced the interpretability of results. Although we elicited three probabilities for each capability, participants provided only one consequence value (the capability of the baseline). That is, participants did not provide a consequence value to represent a "significant improvement" or "significant degradation" from the baseline's capability. Thus, our analysis used systematic assumptions to define values for these consequence values (see the "Analysis" section for assumptions). This approach results in overall expected values that should be interpreted only as *ordinal rankings* of preference. That is, we can conclude only that one alternative is preferred to another; we cannot conclude the magnitude of that preference. Our analyses result in some expected values that appear to be of negligible difference. Although we acknowledge this finding, we cannot conclude that the difference is, in fact, negligible. We can conclude only the order of preference.

Additionally, with only 13 participants, our data analysis is not powerful enough to evaluate whether there is a significant difference in the expected values of different alternatives. Our analysis can only reflect on the results we elicited. That is, our analysis allows us to conclude whether *our participants*, on average, preferred one alternative to another.

Overall Expected Value of the Personnel Concepts

We calculated the mean overall expected value for each alternative across the participants ($n = 13$), on a scale from 0 (lowest value) to 1 (highest value). Figure A.1 shows these results for round 1 (red) and round 2 (blue). For each alternative (including the baseline), participants' mean valuation increased from round 1 to 2, while the variances (shown as standard deviation bars, i.e., a line extending above and below the bars representing the mean value) of their valuations decreased. The latter is a common result of conducting a group discussion, during which agreement tends to increase among participants. Of particular note is the wider variance in participants' evaluation of the baseline in comparison to the other alternatives. This suggests that participants were

Figure A.1
Mean Overall Expected Values of the Alternatives

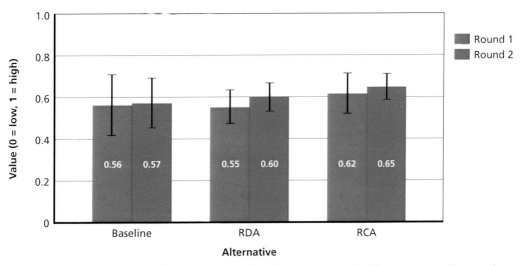

NOTE: Red bars indicate results from round 1, and blue bars from round 2. The error bar at the top of each column indicates the degree of convergence among panel members' assessments in that round.
RAND *RR1065-A.1*

in deeper disagreement about the current personnel management system's capability with respect to the identified objectives. For both rounds, RCA had the highest overall expected value (M = 0.62 in round 1 and M = 0.65 in round 2). However, the ranking of preference for the other alternatives shifted from the first to the second round, with RDA being preferred to the baseline in round 2.

Mean Importance of Objectives

Two measures drive the overall expected values of the alternatives: the evaluation of those alternatives on the eight objectives and the importance (weight) placed on each of those objectives. Figure A.2 shows the mean importance placed on each attribute in rounds 1 (red) and 2 (blue). In both rounds, the four operational objectives (global contingency operations, meeting combatant commands' operational needs, regional security cooperation, and regional contingency operations) were rated as more important (mean importance ≥ 4.1) than the four personnel objectives (recruiting and retention; costs; equity in assignment, selection, and promotion; and other personnel management priorities) (mean importance ≤ 3.6). A comparison of the importance between the first and second rounds reveals that participants' valuations of importance of the attributes changed only slightly, if at all, with costs having the largest shift and being rated as less important in the second round (mean importance = 3.6 in round 1; mean importance = 3.2 in round 2). As with the overall expected-value results, the variance (shown as standard deviation bars) in participants' ratings of importance decreased from the first to second round, which would suggest higher agreement.

Expected Value of Alternatives

Figure A.3 shows the mean expected values of each alternative for each of the eight risk objectives in round 2. The ranking of preferences between the alternatives varies significantly by attribute. The baseline is seen as having the most value in terms of global contingency operations; other personnel management priorities; and equity in assignment, selection, and promotion. RCA is the most preferred in terms of regional contingency operations, costs (where larger expected values represent better or lower costs), and recruiting and retention, with regional security cooperation showing equal value for RDA and RCA. RDA is the most preferred only in terms of meeting combatant commands' operational needs.

Result Sensitivity and Drivers

We performed a set of analyses to explore whether any factors were driving the results of this evaluation. First, as shown in Figure A.4, we calculated separate mean overall expected values for the alternatives in the second round for Army participants (blue, n = 6) and RAND participants (red, n = 6).[3] Army participants had less favorable

---

[3]   We removed the study sponsor from this analysis.

Figure A.2
Mean Importance for Risk Categories

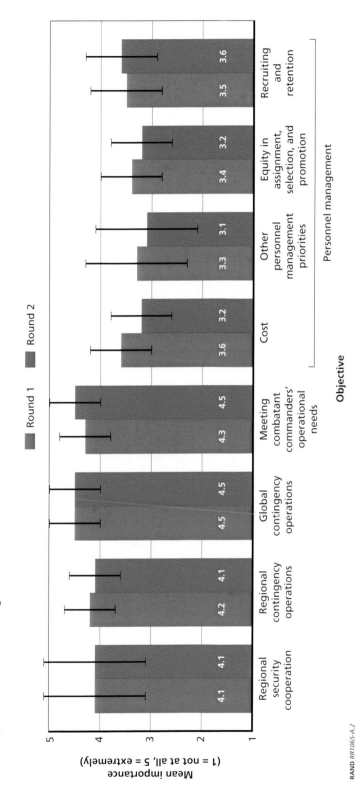

RAND RR1065-A.2

Figure A.3
Mean Expected Values of Alternatives for Risk Categories

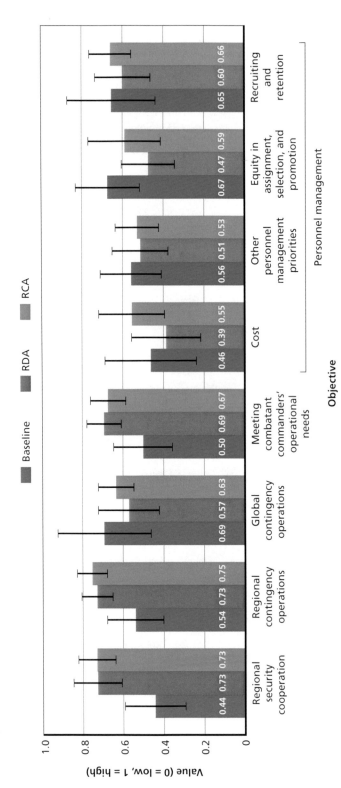

Figure A.4
Mean Expected Values of Alternatives for Army and RAND Participants

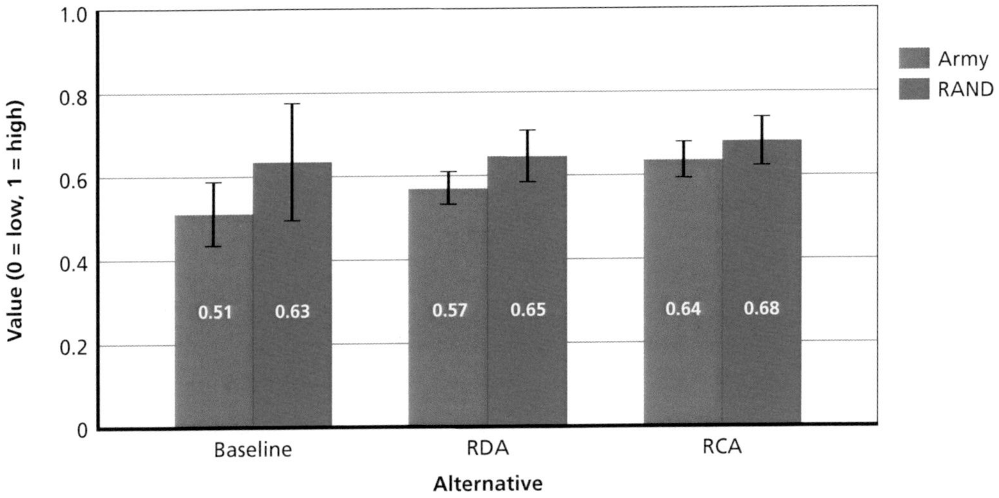

RAND RR1065-A.4

evaluations of all three alternatives. The variance in RAND participants' evaluations (shown as standard deviation bars) is also larger than that for Army participants, suggesting that RAND participants tended to have more disagreement in their evaluations. Overall, both Army and RAND participants held the same preference ranking for the alternatives.

Next, we explored one aspect of sensitivity for RCA's overall expected value. The analysis identifies the percentage reduction in RCA's risk-level expected values that would be necessary for the baseline to be preferred to RCA (in terms of overall expected value). Large reductions would indicate that the overall assessment is robust against changes to the probability and consequence inputs for any one risk objective. Table A.2 shows that the expected value for each RCA risk objective must be reduced by at least 75 percent for the baseline to be preferred to RCA. For three of these objectives, a 100-percent reduction was insufficient to produce an RCA overall expected value that was smaller than that of the baseline. This sensitivity analysis suggests that the RCA overall expected value (and its place as the highest-ranked alternative) is rather insensitive to changes in participants' responses, an indicator of the robustness of the analyses.

**Table A.2
Sensitivity Analysis: Reduction in Objective Value
Required to Change Overall Assessment (for RCA Overall
Expected Value to Be Smaller Than Baseline)**

Objective	Reduction (%)
Regional security cooperation	78
Regional contingency operations	76
Global contingency operations	83
Meeting combatant commands' operational needs	75
Costs	100+[a]
Other personnel management priorities	100+[a]
Equity in assignment, selection, and promotion	100+[a]
Recruiting and retention	97

NOTE: The assessment accounts for changes to the baseline
expected value as a result of parameter changes.

[a] Setting this value to 0 is not sufficient to result in the RCA
expected value being smaller than the baseline.

Bibliography

Allyn, Dan, Jim Huggins, Pat Donahue, Chris Haas, Jeff Talley, Pat Murphy, Olivier Tramond, and Nathan Freier, "Contemporary Military Forum III: Regionally Aligned Forces and Global Engagement," briefing slides, October 18, 2013. As of June 1, 2015:
https://www.ausa.org/meetings/2013/AnnualMeeting/Documents/
Presentation_RegionallyAlignedForcesAnd%20Global%20Engagement.pdf

Army Leader Development Program, *Initiative Summaries, ALDP Charter, 2013 Army Leader Development Strategy, ALDP Priority Lists*, Fort Leavenworth, Kan., Army Leader Development Forum 14-4, August 12, 2014.

Ayyub, Bilal M., *A Practical Guide on Conducting Expert-Opinion Elicitation of Probabilities and Consequences for Corps Facilities*, Alexandria, Va.: U.S. Army Corps of Engineers, Institute for Water Resources Report 01-R-01, January 2001. As of June 1, 2015:
http://www.iwr.usace.army.mil/Portals/70/docs/iwrreports/01-R-01.pdf

Bransford, John B., Ann L. Brown, and Rodney R. Cocking, eds., *How People Learn: Brain, Mind, Experience, and School*, Washington, D.C.: National Academy Press, 1998.

Brooks, Rosa, "Portrait of the Army as a Work in Progress," *Foreign Policy*, Vol. 206, May–June 2014, pp. 42–51. As of June 1, 2015:
http://foreignpolicy.com/2014/05/08/portrait-of-the-army-as-a-work-in-progress/

Brooks, Vincent K., Pat Donahue, Jeff Talley, Michael E. O'Hanlon, and Andrew Krepinevich, "Contemporary Military Forum III, Regionally Aligned Forces: A Globally Responsive and Regionally Engaged Army," briefing slides, October 10, 2014.

Brown, Bernice B., *Delphi Process: A Methodology Used for the Elicitation of Opinions of Experts*, Santa Monica, Calif.: RAND Corporation, P-3925, 1968. As of June 1, 2015:
http://www.rand.org/pubs/papers/P3925.html

Bukowski, Raven, John Childress, Michael J. Colarusso, and David S. Lyle, *Creating an Effective Regional Alignment Strategy for the U.S. Army*, Carlisle Barracks, Pa.: U.S. Army War College Press, November 2014. As of June 1, 2015:
http://www.strategicstudiesinstitute.army.mil/pubs/display.cfm?pubID=1240

Colarusso, Michael J., and David S. Lyle, *Senior Officer Talent Management: Fostering Institutional Adaptability*, Carlisle Barracks, Pa.: U.S. Army War College Press, February 2014. As of June 1, 2015:
http://www.strategicstudiesinstitute.army.mil/pubs/display.cfm?pubID=1188

DA PAM 600-3—*See* U.S. Army, 2014b.

DA PAM 600-25—*See* U.S. Army, 2008.

DA PAM 611-21—*See* U.S. Army, undated (b).

DoD—*See* U.S. Department of Defense.

Ericsson, K. Anders, "The Influence of Experience and Deliberate Practice on the Development of Superior Expert Performance," in K. Anders Ericsson, Neil Charness, Paul J. Feltovich, and Robert R. Hoffman, eds., *The Cambridge Handbook of Expertise and Expert Performance*, Cambridge, UK: Cambridge University Press, 2006, pp. 683–704.

Ericsson, K. Anders, Ralf Th. Krampe, and Clemens Tesch-Römer, "The Role of Deliberate Practice in the Acquisition of Expert Performance," *Psychological Review*, Vol. 100, No. 3, 1993, pp. 363–406.

Field, Kimberly, James Learmont, and Jason Charland, "Regionally Aligned Forces: Business *Not* as Usual," *Parameters,* Vol. 43, No. 3, Autumn 2013, pp. 55–63. As of June 1, 2015:
http://www.strategicstudiesinstitute.army.mil/pubs/Parameters/issues/Autumn_2013/5_Field.pdf

Gates, Robert M., *Quadrennial Defense Review Report*, Washington, D.C.: U.S. Department of Defense, February 2010. As of July 4, 2015:
http://www.defense.gov/qdr/images/QDR_as_of_12Feb10_1000.pdf

Grigsby, Wayne W., Jr., Patrick Matlock, Christopher R. Norrie, and Karen Radka, "Mission Command in the Regionally Aligned Division Headquarters," *Military Review*, Vol. 93, No. 6, November–December 2013, pp. 3–9. As of June 1, 2015:
http://usacac.army.mil/CAC2/MilitaryReview/Archives/English/
MilitaryReview_20131231_art004.pdf

Joint Base Lewis-McChord Language and Culture Center, "Language/Culture Training Models," briefing slides, June 6, 2014. As of June 1, 2015:
http://govtilr.org/Publications/ILR%20Presentation%206JUN14%20Plenary.pdf

JP 1-02—*See* U.S. Joint Chiefs of Staff, 2012a.

Klein, Gary A., *Sources of Power: How People Make Decisions*, Cambridge, Mass.: MIT Press, 1999.

Lord, Robert G., and Karen J. Maher, "Cognitive Theory in Industrial and Organizational Psychology," in Marvin D. Dunnette and Leaetta M. Hough, eds., *Handbook of Industrial and Organizational Psychology*, Vol. 2, Palo Alto, Calif.: Consulting Psychologists Press, 1991, pp. 1–62.

Markel, M. Wade, Henry A. Leonard, Charlotte Lynch, Christina Panis, Peter Schirmer, and Carra S. Sims, *Developing U.S. Army Officers' Capabilities for Joint, Interagency, Intergovernmental, and Multinational Environments*, Santa Monica, Calif.: RAND Corporation, MG-990-A, 2011. As of June 1, 2015:
http://www.rand.org/pubs/monographs/MG990.html

McHugh, John M., and Raymond T. Odierno, *2014 Army Posture Statement*, Washington, D.C.: Headquarters, Department of the Army, April 2014. As of June 1, 2015:
http://usarmy.vo.llnwd.net/e2/rv5_downloads/aps/aps_2014.pdf

McLeary, Paul, "Army's Pacific Pathways: New Tactics, Lessons Learned," *DefenseNews*, October 13, 2014a. As of October 28, 2014:
http://www.defensenews.com/article/20141013/SHOWSCOUT04/310130028/
Army-s-Pacific-Pathways-New-Tactics-Lessons-Learned

———, "Interview: Lt. Gen. Stephen Lanza, Commander, US Army's I Corps," *DefenseNews*, October 22, 2014b. As of October 28, 2014:
http://www.defensenews.com/article/20141022/DEFREG02/310220046/
Interview-Lt-Gen-Stephen-Lanza

McMaster, Herbert R., "Maneuver Center of Excellence Language, Regional Expertise, and Culture (LREC) Program Guidance," memorandum for chief, Training Development Division, Directorate of Training Development, Maneuver Center of Excellence, Fort Benning, Ga., August 19, 2013. As of June 1, 2015:
http://www.benning.army.mil/mcoe/maneuverconference/2013/content/pdf/TDD%20-%20Memo%20-%20%20LREC%20Strategy%20Document%20Dated%2019%20Aug%202013.pdf

Mirikelam, François, "Summary of Conference Proceedings, Operation Serval: The Return of Deep Attack Operations by Land and Air Forces," *Réflexions Tactiques*, Special Edition, 2014.

Mouton, Daniel E., "The Army's Foreign Area Officer Program: To Wither or to Improve?" *Army*, Vol. 61, No. 3, March 2011, pp. 21–24. As of June 1, 2015:
http://www.ausa.org/publications/armymagazine/archive/2011/3/documents/fc_mouton_0311.pdf

Norman, Geoff, Kevin Eva, Lee Brooks, and Stan Hamstra, "Expertise in Medicine and Surgery," in K. Anders Ericsson, Neil Charness, Paul J. Feltovich, and Robert R. Hoffman, eds., *The Cambridge Handbook of Expertise and Expert Performance*, Cambridge, UK: Cambridge University Press, 2006, pp. 339–354.

Odierno, Raymond T., and John M. McHugh, *Army Strategic Planning Guidance 2013*, Washington, D.C.: Headquarters, Department of the Army, 2013. As of June 1, 2015:
http://www.chapnet.army.mil/pdf/ASPG%202013-4%20Feb%2012.pdf

OEMA—*See* Office of Economic and Manpower Analysis.

Office of Economic and Manpower Analysis, *Army Green Pages Proof-of-Concept Pilot Report: Using Regulated Market Mechanisms to Manage Officer Talent*, October 1, 2012.

Olsen, Wyatt, "Pacific Pathways: Army Prepares New Tack for Deploying Forces in Pacific," *Stars and Stripes*, May 1, 2014a. As of October 29, 2014:
http://www.stripes.com/news/pacific-pathways-army-prepares-new-tack-for-deploying-forces-in-pacific-1.280623

———, "Army's Pacific Pathways Deployment Concept Kicks Off in Indonesia," *Stars and Stripes*, September 28, 2014b. As of June 1, 2015:
http://www.stripes.com/news/army-s-pacific-pathways-deployment-concept-kicks-off-in-indonesia-1.305455

Panetta, Leon E., *Sustaining U.S. Global Leadership: Priorities for 21st Century Defense*, Washington, D.C.: U.S. Department of Defense, January 2012. As of June 1, 2015:
http://www.defense.gov/news/Defense_Strategic_Guidance.pdf

Project GO, "Policies: Army ROTC Policies and Initiatives," undated. As of October 29, 2014:
http://www.rotcprojectgo.org/policies/army

Ripley, Amanda, "What Makes a Great Teacher?" *Atlantic*, January–February 2010. As of June 3, 2015:
http://www.theatlantic.com/magazine/archive/2010/01/what-makes-a-great-teacher/307841/

Sackman, Harold, *Delphi Assessment: Expert Opinion, Forecasting, and Group Process*, Santa Monica, Calif.: RAND Corporation, R-1283-PR, 1974. As of June 1, 2015:
http://www.rand.org/pubs/reports/R1283.html

Savage, Leonard J., *The Foundations of Statistics*, New York: Wiley, 1954.

SOUTHCOM officials—*See* U.S. Southern Command officials.

Tan, Michelle, "U.S. Commits BCT to NATO Rotation," *Army Times*, July 22, 2013a. As of October 29, 2014:
http://www.armytimes.com/article/20130722/
NEWS/307220008/U-S-commits-BCT-NATO-rotation

———, "First Regionally Aligned BCT Shares Lessons Learned," *Army Times*, September 16, 2013b. As of October 28, 2014:
http://www.armytimes.com/article/20130916/NEWS08/309160009/
First-regionally-aligned-BCT-shares-lessons-learned

Truesdell, Bryan P., "Balance Within the Rebalance: The Supporting Role of the U.S. Military in the Asia–Pacific Region," Honolulu: Asia Pacific Center for Security Studies, June 2014. As of June 1, 2015:
http://www.apcss.org/wp-content/uploads/2014/06/Truesdell-Rebalance-2014.pdf

Under Secretary of Defense for Personnel and Readiness, *Department of Defense Strategic Plan for Language Skills, Regional Expertise, and Cultural Capabilities, 2011–2016*, Washington, D.C.: U.S. Department of Defense, undated. As of June 1, 2015:
http://prhome.defense.gov/Portals/52/Documents/RFM/Readiness/DLNSEO/files/
STRAT%20PLAN.pdf

U.S. Army, "Careers and Jobs: Interpreter/Translator (09L)," undated (a). As of February 24, 2015:
http://www.goarmy.com/careers-and-jobs/browse-career-and-job-categories/
intelligence-and-combat-support/interpreter-translator.html

———, *Military Occupational Classification and Structure*, Washington, D.C.: Headquarters, Department of the Army, Pamphlet 611-21, undated (b); referenced June 30, 2015.

———, *U.S. Army Noncommissioned Officer Professional Development Guide*, Washington, D.C.: Headquarters, Department of the Army, Pamphlet 600-25, July 28, 2008. As of June 1, 2015:
http://www.apd.army.mil/pdffiles/p600_25.pdf

———, *Army Culture and Foreign Language Strategy*, Washington, D.C.: Headquarters, Department of the Army, December 1, 2009. As of June 1, 2015:
http://www.alu.army.mil/ALU_DOCS/
Army%20Culture%20%20Foreign%20Language%20Strategy%20Final.pdf

———, Fort Hood Press Center, "1st Cav's Ironhorse Brigade to Support Operation Atlantic Resolve in Europe," press release, August 14, 2014a. As of October 29, 2014:
http://www.forthoodpresscenter.com/go/doc/3439/2225270/

———, *Commissioned Officer Professional Development and Career Management*, Washington, D.C.: Headquarters, Department of the Army, Pamphlet 600-3, December 3, 2014b. As of July 4, 2015:
http://www.apd.army.mil/pdffiles/p600_3.pdf

U.S. Army Africa, "Overview Brief for the Army Training and Leader Development Conference, 10–12 July 2013," briefing slides, c. 2013.

U.S. Army Africa official, interview with Lisa Saum-Manning, Carlisle Barracks, Pa., August 18, 2014.

U.S. Army Cadet Command, "The Cultural Understanding and Language Proficiency (CULP) Program," undated. As of October 29, 2014:
http://www.cadetcommand.army.mil/culp/

U.S. Army Combined Arms Center, "TRADOC Culture Center," last reviewed March 31, 2015; referenced July 7, 2015. As of July 17, 2015:
http://usacac.army.mil/organizations/cace/tcc

U.S. Army Command and General Staff College official, telephone interview with Jonathan Welch, August 19, 2014.

U.S. Army Europe, *USAREUR 2020: Prevent, Shape, Win*, Wiesbaden, Germany: U.S. Army Europe, version 1.2, May 28, 2014. As of October 27, 2014:
http://www.eur.army.mil/2020/files/USAREUR_2020_v1-2_28May2014.pdf

U.S. Army Europe official, telephone interview with Lisa Saum-Manning, August 26, 2014.

U.S. Army official, interview with Jonathan Welch, Command and General Staff College, August 19, 2014.

U.S. Army South official 1, interview with Lisa Saum-Manning, Guatemala City, May 13, 2014.

U.S. Army South official 2, telephone interview with Lisa Saum-Manning, July 17, 2014.

U.S. Army War College, Department of Distance Education, "Curriculum," undated. As of October 29, 2014:
https://dde.carlisle.army.mil/curriculum.cfm

U.S. Central Command officials, telephone interviews with Lisa Saum-Manning, August 4, 14, and 27, 2014.

U.S. Department of Defense, "Operation Atlantic Resolve: America's Continued Commitment to European Security," undated. As of October 28, 2014:
http://www.defense.gov/home/features/2014/0514_atlanticresolve/

———, *National Defense Strategy*, Washington, D.C., June 2008. As of June 1, 2015:
http://permanent.access.gpo.gov/lps103291/2008%20national%20defense%20strategy.pdf

———, "Joint Qualification System (JQS) Primer," February 2013. As of March 2, 2015:
http://www.jdtc.eustis.army.mil/rss/OpenRSS.aspx?docid=405

———, *Quadrennial Defense Review 2014*, Washington, D.C., March 4, 2014a. As of June 1, 2015:
http://www.defense.gov/pubs/2014_Quadrennial_Defense_Review.pdf

———, "Military Accessions Vital to National Interest (MAVNI) Program Eligibility," November 2014b. As of February 24, 2015:
http://www.defense.gov/news/mavni-fact-sheet.pdf

U.S. European Command, Communication and Engagement Directorate, "Operation Atlantic Resolve," August 28, 2014. As of October 29, 2014:
http://www.defense.gov/home/features/2014/0514_atlanticresolve/FactSheet_28Aug14.pdf

U.S. Government Accountability Office, *Security Force Assistance: The Army and Marine Corps Have Ongoing Efforts to Identify and Track Advisors, but the Army Needs a Plan to Capture Advising Experience: Report to Congressional Committees*, Washington, D.C., GAO-14-482, July 2014. As of August 17, 2015:
http://www.gao.gov/products/GAO-14-482

U.S. Joint Chiefs of Staff, *Joint Training Manual for the Armed Forces of the United States*, Washington, D.C., Chairman of the Joint Chiefs of Staff Manual 3500.03A, September 1, 2002.

———, *Department of Defense Dictionary of Military and Associated Terms*, Washington, D.C., *Joint Publication 1-02*, 2012a.

———, *Capstone Concept for Joint Operations: Joint Force 2020*, Washington, D.C., September 10, 2012b. As of June 1, 2015:
http://www.dtic.mil/doctrine/concepts/ccjo_jointforce2020.pdf

USMA—*See* U.S. Military Academy.

U.S. Military Academy, West Point, "International Cadets," undated (a). As of February 26, 2015:
http://www.usma.edu/admissions/sitepages/pros_cadets_international.aspx

————, Department of Foreign Languages, "Semester-Abroad Fellow Program: 'West Point's Signature International Program,'" undated (b). As of February 26, 2015:
http://www.usma.edu/dfl/SitePages/Semester%20Abroad%20Fellow%20Program.aspx

U.S. Southern Command officials, interviews with Lisa Saum-Manning, May 1 and 17, 2014.

Vergun, David, "Regionally Aligned Forces Continue to Organize Despite Budget Uncertainties," U.S. Army, October 23, 2013. As of March 3, 2015:
http://www.army.mil/article/113660/
Regionally_aligned_forces_continue_to_organize_despite_budget_uncertainties/

Von Neumann, John, and Oskar Morgenstern, *Theory of Games and Economic Behavior*, 2nd ed., Princeton, N.J.: Princeton University Press, 1947.